THE

PASTORAL

EPISTLES

THE
PASTORAL
EPISTLES

A Commentary on I & II Timothy & Titus

BY J. R. ENSEY

The Pastoral Epistles
A Commentary on I and II Timothy and Titus

by J. R. Ensey

©1990 Word Aflame Press
Hazelwood, MO 63042-2299

Cover Design by Tim Agnew

Printed in United States of America

Printed by

Library of Congress Cataloging-in-Publication Data

Ensey, J. R.
    The Pastoral Epistles: a commentary on I and II Timothy and Titus /J. R. Ensey.
        p. cm.
    Includes bibliographical references.
    ISBN 0-932581-69-2
    1. Bible. N.T. Pastoral Epistles—Commentaries. I. Bible. N.T. Pastoral Epistles. English. Authorized. 1990. II. Title.
BS2735.3.E57   1990
227'.83077—dc20
                                                    90-35717
                                                    CIP

To all those students who have patiently and graciously received these practical lessons in the Texas Bible College classrooms and subsequently put them into practice in many fields of ministry.

Contents

General Introduction
to
The Pastoral Epistles

The apostle Paul authored three letters, or epistles, to two of his younger colleagues whom he affectionately referred to as his "sons." These young men were pastors and evangelists who labored with him in his ministerial endeavors. He would often leave them in charge of assemblies in cities where he had gathered together a congregation. They would usually rejoin him at some point on another missionary journey.

During these periods when they were left in charge, he corresponded with them to encourage them to be strong in defense of the gospel, admonish them to faithfulness, and offer specific instructions for both them and various elements of the church. This correspondence was inspired of God and was accepted as canonical by the early church. It was viewed as a general pattern for ministerial activity and the operation of local churches everywhere.

These epistles were apparently used by Polycarp, Justin Martyr, and Irenaeus during the second century. Only Marcion (c. A. D. 140) is known to have rejected them, accepting the canonicity of only ten Pauline epistles and Luke's Gospel. The Muratorian Fragment (c. 170-200) mentions Paul's letters to seven churches and adds: "But he wrote one letter to Philemon, and one to Titus, and two to Timothy from affection and love."

The churches Timothy and Titus pastored were young churches, most of them no more than a few years old. They struggled with church polity, false teachers, aberrant philosophies, immorality, and social problems. We face many of the same issues today, which makes these writings particularly relevant for us. No doubt Timothy and Titus welcomed these letters as a breath of fresh air, as light in a shadowed place, as water in a dry land. The Gnostic influence, the Judaizers, and heretics like Alexander were matters that would have been difficult to handle without a word of advice from their mentor.

The departure from vintage Pauline style forms the basis for the only serious challenge to the authorship of Paul. The style does vary considerably from other Pauline writings, that of Romans being the most closely related to the Pastorals. As Vincent said, "We miss the unclosed parenthesis, the sudden digressions, the obscurities arising from the headlong impetus of thought and feeling. The construction of sentences is simple, the thoughts are expressed without momentum or color." Without doubt Paul took into consideration his reader and the present situation, and then couched his instructions in language that best expressed his mood.

Some critics complain that entire families of words widely used by Paul in his other epistles are missing here and that there are many terms employed in the Pastorals alone. But these were private letters written under particular circumstances and perhaps by different scribes. Paul may have written some letters with his own hand

(Galatians 6:11), but possibly due to failing eyesight, he most likely employed scribes or secretaries such as Luke to do much of the actual writing. Just as God uses an individual's own faculties and speech variations in the oral gifts of the Spirit, the writers employed by Paul may have drawn from their own training to help him choose the right words and grammatical structure to convey his divinely inspired message accurately. If so, that does not detract in any way from the authenticity, divine inspiration, or accuracy of the documents. In a similar way, one may note differences among the Gospel writers as they described the same scenes.

In any case, the early post-apostolic church gratefully accepted these epistles as authentic and worthy of canonization. They have proven their worth over the centuries and are loved today by all who embrace truth and righteousness. Only the skeptic, who would just as soon not hear the things Paul had to say about heresies and heretics, finds fault with these practical instructions to two young preachers of the first century.

THE FIRST EPISTLE OF PAUL THE APOSTLE TO

TIMOTHY

Introduction To First Timothy

The Author

The writer of this epistle introduced himself as "Paul, an apostle of Jesus Christ . . . unto Timothy, my own son in the faith" (1:1-2). Conservative scholars accept Paul's authorship of this letter. (See the General Introduction for a response to critics on this point.)

The Recipient

Timothy was discipled in Christianity and trained in public ministry by the apostle Paul. He was from Lystra and was probably converted during Paul's first missionary journey (Acts 14:6-21; 16:1-2). His father was an unbelieving Greek, but his mother, Eunice, and his grandmother, Lois, were godly Hebrew women (Acts 16:1; II Timothy 1:5). They had nurtured him on the Scriptures, and evidently his heart had been good ground for the seed of the Word of God (II Timothy 3:14-15). His life was one of dedicated service and fruitfulness.

On Paul's second missionary journey he invited Timothy to join the missionary team, which consisted of Paul, Luke, and Silas (Acts 16:3). Some have suggested that Timothy was chosen to take John Mark's place (Acts 13:5). Paul had Timothy circumcised so that the Jews would not be offended when the missionaries came to preach among them and visit their synagogues (Acts 16:3). Paul and the presbytery formally ordained the young preacher (I Timothy 4:14; II Timothy 1:6). He became like a son to Paul, perhaps his closest associate throughout his ministry, and was a close companion during his first imprisonment (Philippians 1:1; Colossians 1:1; Philemon 1:1). He apparently suffered incarceration himself at some point (Hebrews 13:23).

Timothy served at least five churches, including Thessalonica (I Thessalonians 3:2, 6), Corinth (I Corinthians 4:17), Philippi (Philippians 2:19-23), Berea (Acts 17:13-14), and Ephesus (I Timothy 1:3). He was at Ephesus when he received this communication from Paul.

Timothy's age is generally believed to be above thirty-five years at the time of this writing. (See the commentary on 4:12.)

Place and Date of Writing

This letter was probably written about A.D. 62 or 63 between Paul's first and second imprisonment. Acts 28:16, 30 describes Paul's first incarceration in Rome, during which time he wrote Philippians, Colossians, Ephesians, and Philemon. In these epistles he spoke of his hope for a soon release (Philippians 1:23-25; 2:24; Philemon 22). He was evidently released to make a planned trip to Spain (Romans 15:24), and in II Timothy 4:7 he said he had finished his course.

From I Timothy 1:3 we may assume that Paul was in Macedonia when he wrote this letter. It is likely that after his release from his first Roman imprisonment he made a visit to Ephesus, and finding certain spiritual discrepancies there, he left Timothy to serve as a presiding elder, or pastor, and to set some things in order (1:3-4).

Emphases

The epistle is pastoral from beginning to end. It is from one minister to another. It is full of "preacher talk." The letter details conditions that should prevail in a New Testament church. It outlines the duties and responsibilities of the ministry along with virtually every social and age group in the assembly. Handling pastoral problems is a general theme.

One major emphasis is to encourage Timothy to intercept and denounce the purveyors of false teachings (1:3-4; 4:1-3; 6:3-4). He was to "take heed unto . . . the doctrine" (4:16). No church is stronger than the message it embraces.

Another focal point of this epistle is the outstanding passage on the dangers of materialism (6:6-19). It appeals for contentment as opposed to covetousness and greed. It places money and wealth in its proper perspective (6:17-19), saying, "For the love of money is the root of all evil" (6:10).

Outline of
First Timothy

I. The Salutation (1:1-2)

II. Personal Exhortations (1:3-20)
    A. To Protect the Purity of the Gospel (1:3-11)
        1. From fables and genealogies (4-5)
        2. From the corruption of false teachers (6-7)
        3. From sinners and profane persons (8-11)
    B. To Remember Paul's Personal Experience (1:12-17)
        1. He had been an injurious blasphemer (12-13)
        2. He considered himself the chief of sinners (14-15)
        3. He obtained grace for which he glorified God (16-17)
    C. To Guard against Corruption of the Faith (1:18-20)
        1. Remember the prophecies (18)
        2. The results of departing from the faith (19)
        3. The judgment of certain blasphemers (20)

III. General Exhortations (2:1-15)
    A. To Pray for Others (2:1-8)

      1. For all men (1)
      2. For civic leaders (2a)
      3. Purpose of the prayers (2b-8)
   B. For the Woman to Serve with Meekness
     and Submission (2:9-15)
      1. Her apparel (9)
      2. Her attitude (9-11)
      3. Her authority (12-15)

IV. Divine Order for the Church and the Ministry
   (3:1-16)
   A. Qualifications for Ministerial Leadership
     (3:1-7)
      1. Character (1-3)
      2. Relationships (4-6)
      3. Reputation (7)
   B. Qualifications for Lay Leadership (3:8-12)
      1. Personal qualifications (8-9)
      2. Tests to prove worthiness to serve (10)
      3. Stipulations for wives (11)
      4. Domestic qualifications (12)
   C. Rewards for Christian Service (3:13)
   D. Personal Insights for Timothy (3:14-16)
      1. These writings precede Paul's visit (14)
      2. How to operate in the framework of the
         body (15)
      3. The heart of the church's doctrine (16)

V. Specific Advice to a Young Minister (4:1-16)
   A. Concerning the Coming Apostasy (4:1-5)
      1. The prediction of the problems (1)
      2. The nature of the apostates (2)

> 3. The doctrine of the apostates (3a)
> 4. The refutation of the doctrines (3b-5)
> B. The Defense against Apostasy (4:6-11)
> 1. A faithful ministry (6)
> 2. Refusal of fables (7)
> 3. A clear understanding of Christian doctrine (8-11)
> C. Perseverance in Good Works (4:12-16)
> 1. Provide a visible model of Christianity (12-13)
> 2. Develop personal gifts (14)
> 3. Meditate on truth (15)
> 4. Continue in the doctrine (16)

VI. Official Work with Specific Groups (5:1-25)
  A. Treatment of Various Segments of the Church (5:1-16)
   1. Older men (1)
   2. Older women (2)
   3. Widows (3-16)
  B. Honoring Elders (5:17-18)
   1. Worthy of double honor (17)
   2. Deserving of the benefits of ministry (18)
  C. Discipline of Elders (5:19-21)
   1. The accusation (19)
   2. The rebuke (20)
   3. The appeal for impartiality (21)
  D. Advice Concerning Ordination of Elders (5:22)
   1. Be slow to ordain (22a)
   2. Do not share in failings of others (22b)
   3. Maintain personal purity (22c)

E. Perspectives on Health and Sin (5:23-25)
1. The use of wine for medicinal purposes (23)
2. The sins judged beforehand (24)
3. Good works also obvious (25)

VII. The Believer's Economic Relationships (6:1-10)
A. Relationships of Slaves and Masters (6:1-2)
1. Respect for masters (1a)
2. Proper attitudes protect the reputation of the church (1b)
3. Dual responsibility toward believing masters (2)
B. The Source of Worldly Values (6:3-5)
1. Conceited teachers (3-4a)
2. Controversies and arguments (4b)
3. False doctrine that financial gain is indicative of godliness (5)
C. Godliness with Contentment (6:6-10)
1. Acceptance of our earthly status (6-8)
2. The desire for riches (9a)
3. Results of greed (9b-10)

VIII. A Final Charge (6:11-21)
A. Alternatives to Materialism (6:11-12)
1. Flee greed and love of gain (11a)
2. Pursue the fulfillment of righteousness (11b)
3. Grasp eternal things that serve one's purpose (12)
B. Adjuration of Paul (6:13-16)
1. To keep the commandment to remain free from greed (13-14)

2. God is called as a witness (13)
3. Duration of the charge (14)
4. The all-seeing Christ will have power to reward faithfulness (15-16)

C. Warn the Wealthy (6:17-19)
  1. To guard against misplaced trust (17)
  2. To manifest good works (18)
  3. To plan for the future (19)

D. Reject Worldly Philosophies (6:20-21a)
  1. Hold on to truth (20a)
  2. Avoid teachers who are worldly-wise (20b)
  3. The results of such philosophies (21a)

E. The Benediction (6:21b)

I TIMOTHY
Chapter One

The introductory remarks of the apostle Paul to Timothy are quite abbreviated, perhaps because of their close association and regular contact. Since this letter is personal, Paul felt no obligation to include greetings to or from other individuals or groups as was the case with Romans, Corinthians, and other epistles. Paul seemed to be heavily burdened and deeply concerned about a number of issues with which Timothy was involved, so he launched quickly into the discussion of those matters.

I. Salutation (1:1-2)

(1) Paul, an apostle of Jesus Christ by the commandment of God our Saviour, and Lord Jesus Christ, which is our hope; (2) unto Timothy, my own son in the faith: Grace, mercy, and peace, from God our Father and Jesus Christ our Lord.

Paul's first words were typical of his openings: "Paul, an apostle of Jesus Christ. . . ." Should the letter be lost, the finder could easily determine both the writer and the addressee. The only exception to this pattern among New Testament epistles is the letter to the Hebrews and the letters of John.

Verse 1. Paul stated clearly that he was an apostle (one chosen and sent bearing credentials and authority) by the direct commandment of God (Galatians 1:11-12; I Corinthians 1:1). He was not self-called, self-ordained, or self-appointed. His apostleship was certified and confirmed by the church in Antioch (Acts 13:1-4; 14:14) and by representatives of the original Twelve (Galatians 2:7-9). He received his commission as an apostle to the Gentiles from the Lord Himself (Galatians 1:1, 15-16). He made an elaborate defense of his right to the title by submitting his record of faithfulness to the cause (II Corinthians 11:5; 13:6).

Paul assumed the Gentile version of his Hebrew name, Saul, since he was now called to be an apostle unto the Gentiles. The name Paul is a derivative of the Latin *paulus,* which means "little." This name may be a clue to Paul's stature, to which he seems to allude in II Corinthians 10:1, 10. Although his body may have had its problems, his heart was not *paulus* nor frail! The apocryphal second-century work *Acts of Paul and Thecla* describes Paul's physical appearance this way: "A man small of stature, with a bald head and crooked legs, in a good state of body, with eyebrows meeting and nose somewhat hooked" (3).

The use of the official title *apostolos* may indicate that this letter was more than just a personal note but was intended for publication and reading in the assemblies visited by Timothy. (See the commentary on I Timothy 4:13.)

"Of Jesus Christ." Some texts invert the order to state the office first and the formal name later ("Christ Jesus"). Christ, or *Christos,* is the equivalent of the

Hebrew *Messiah,* both meaning "the anointed one."
Wuest explained the significance of this name here:

In a Jewish setting such as the Gospel according-
ing to Matthew, the word [Christ] refers to the
Messiah of Israel, the Anointed of God who is to
become its King. In a Church setting, as here in
First Timothy, it had the significance, not of the
covenanted King of Israel, but of The Anointed One
of God, to Paul and his Greek readers. The name
"Jesus" is the English spelling of the Greek word
Iesous, which in turn is the Greek spelling of the
Hebrew word we know in its transliterated form as
"Jehoshua," the "h" disappearing, since the Greek
language has no letter "h." The Hebrew word
means "Jehovah saves." This was its significance
to Paul and his Greek readers. In the latter name,
we see the deity, incarnation, and substitutionary
atonement of our Lord, for the Jehovah of the Old
Testament could not save lost sinners unless He
paid the price of their sins, thus satisfying His
justice, the price being outpoured blood, since the
penalty of sin is death.[1]

Since no punctuation appeared in early Greek
manuscripts, the King James Version translators inserted
it where they felt it was critical to smooth reading and
improved clarity. Probably the clearest way to write the
combination name and title would be Christ Jesus (like
"President Smith") or Jesus, Christ. Since Peter said to
Jesus, "Thou art the Christ" (Matthew 16:16), it would
not do violence to the nomenclature or the doctrine of

Christ to refer to Him as Jesus, the Christ. Jesus was His name; Christ was His office.

Applying that approach, it is unlikely that the phrase "and Lord Jesus Christ" should be set off by commas. Understanding the Godhead as Paul did (I Timothy 3:16), and the office and titles claimed by Christ, he was simply saying, "Paul, an apostle of Christ Jesus by the commandment of God our Saviour and Lord, Christ Jesus." It is doctrinally impossible to separate Lord and God: "The LORD is God, and . . . there is none else" (I Kings 8:60). (See also Mark 12:29; Acts 9:5; Ephesians 4:4-6.)

If Paul was trying to acknowledge separate persons in the Godhead in the greeting, why the omission of the Holy Spirit? Obviously, such acknowledgement was not his purpose since he called Jesus "the only wise God" in I Timothy 1:17 and spoke of "the doctrine of God our Saviour" in Titus 2:10. (See also Jude 25.) Because the verse uses *and (kai)* between these titles and names does not mean that they refer to different persons. I Thessalonians 1:3 and 3:11 speak of "God and Father," yet no one says they are two persons. Any time the Bible mentions God or the Father, it recognizes the Holy Spirit, because they are one and the same. Separate mention of Christ simply serves to keep focus on His role as Son in redemption.

David Bernard provided further insight on these greeting passages:

> The word translated "and" is from the Greek word *kai*. It can be translated as "and" or as "even" (in the sense of "that is" or "which is the same as"). For example, the KJV translates *kai* as "and"

in II Corinthians 1:2 but as "even" in verse 3. Verse 2 says, "From God our Father, and from the Lord Jesus Christ," while verse 3 says, "God, even the Father of our Lord Jesus Christ." Verse 2 could properly appear as, "From God our Father, even from the Lord Jesus Christ." The KJV translates *kai* as "even" in several other places, including the phrases "God, even the Father" (I Corinthians 15:24; James 3:9) and "God, even our Father" (I Thessalonians 3:13). So the greetings could read just as easily, "From God our Father, even the Lord Jesus Christ." To further support this, the Greek does not have the definite article "the" before "Lord Jesus Christ" in any of the salutations. Thus, even if we translate *kai* as "and," the phrases literally read, "From God our Father and Lord Jesus Christ." Even when the translations render *kai* as "and" they often agree that the phrase denotes only one being or person.[2]

According to Greek rules, a definite article must precede both nouns in order to indicate different persons, objects, or things. And in I Timothy 5:21 and II Timothy 4:1 the Greek text clearly identifies God and Jesus as one and the same being.

This verse calls Jesus "our hope." He is similarly identified in Colossians 1:27 and in Titus 2:13. This designation emphasizes that Christ is the object of our hope. We trust in His vicarious death (Romans 5:8), His victorious resurrection (I Peter 3:21), and His intercession for us by His sacrifice (Hebrews 7:25). Our hope of being resurrected is inextricably linked to the fact of His resurrection (I Corinthians 15:12-20). Our hope is that someday we will have a body "like unto his glorious body" (Philippians 3:21) and will in that way be like Him (I John 3:2).

Verse 2. Timothy was Paul's "adopted" son and he treated him as his own. Evidently Paul played a vital role in Timothy's Christian development and possibly even his salvation experience. He provided the nurture, along with Timothy's mother, Eunice, and grandmother, Lois, to bring him to spiritual maturity (II Timothy 1:5). Paul had seen positive potential in him early on that merited the investment of time. This investment had paid off by bringing Timothy to a trusted position in the circle of Paul's friends and emissaries (I Corinthians 4:17; Philippians 2:19-22).

Paul used the word *gnesios* (own) to connote "true, genuine, not spurious." Titus 1:4 uses the same word used in reference to Titus: "mine own son after the common faith." Timothy was probably converted in his late teenage years and was approximately twenty-three or twenty-four years of age on Paul's second visit to Lystra. (See the commentary on 4:12.)

"Grace" is unmerited favor bestowed by God. In ancient Greece, grace *(charis)* was a favor done for a fellow Greek (not an enemy) without hope of return. But in the New Testament, grace takes on deeper meaning since God extends the benefits of Calvary to His enemies, not merely to His friends (Titus 2:11; John 19:37; Acts 2:23).

"Mercy" appears in none of Paul's salutations except the letters to Timothy and Titus, and some manuscripts even omit it from Titus. This attribute is compassionate love, open-handed dealing, and protective kindness. Mercy is what Christ brought to us through Calvary, and it serves to stand between us and sure judgment. Mercy instead of justice is the clearest expression of God's love (John 3:16).

"Peace" *(eirene)* according to Wuest is "that which has been bound together again after having been separated." Separation renders confusion, anxiety, and misery in one's life. When Christ comes in by invitation, He brings a "peace . . . which passeth all understanding" (Philippians 4:7). He puts things together, mends the broken relationships, and provides a tranquility for the spirit.

These blessings, then, Paul wished upon Timothy. He also explained their source—they are from "God our Father and Jesus Christ our Lord." This phrase emphasizes the Sonship ministry of Christ as the true basis of these blessings. The combined action of God the Father (Spirit) and Christ Jesus (the Son, flesh, expression, manifestation) has brought to us this "so great salvation" (Hebrews 2:3). (See John 1:1-4; I Timothy 3:16; Hebrews 1:3.)

II. Personal Exhortations (1:3-20)

A. To Protect the Purity of the Gospel (1:3-11)

(3) As I besought thee to abide still at Ephesus, when I went into Macedonia, that thou mightest charge some that they teach no other doctrine, (4) neither give heed to fables and endless genealogies, which minister questions, rather than godly edifying which is in faith: so do. (5) Now the end of the commandment is charity out of a pure heart, and of a good conscience, and of faith unfeigned: (6) from which some having swerved have turned aside unto vain jangling; (7) desiring to be teachers of the law; understand-

*ing neither what they say, nor whereof they affirm. (8) But
we know that the law is good, if a man use it lawfully;
(9) knowing this, that the law is not made for a righteous
man, but for the lawless and disobedient, for the ungodly
and for sinners, for unholy and profane, for murderers
of fathers and murderers of mothers, for manslayers,
(10) for whoremongers, for them that defile themselves with
mankind, for menstealers, for liars, for perjured persons,
and if there be any other thing that is contrary to sound
doctrine; (11) according to the glorious gospel of the blessed God, which was committed to my trust.*

Verse 3. Paul reminded Timothy of a former dictum,
whether given verbally or written we are not told, that
he had shared with him on some occasion. The apostle
desired him to remain at Ephesus. The strength of the
Greek word translated "besought" indicates that Paul
sincerely pleaded with him to continue his service in that
city. Paul evidently had traveled to Macedonia with
Timothy, leaving him there to continue to "do the work
of an evangelist" (II Timothy 4:5) and strengthen the
assembly.

Paul implored Timothy to warn "some" that they
were to teach nothing contrary to the true doctrine. They
were to be charged to remain faithful to the apostolic
message. No different doctrines were to be tolerated. This
statement corresponds with Paul's appeal to the Corinthians that they "all speak the same thing" (I Corinthians
1:10). A few then as now probably scoffed at such a suggestion, considering such a possibility quite unrealistic.
While we may not agree on every idea, unity of doctrine
should always remain the ideal for which we strive.

Verse 4. Not only were there to be no variations on the core themes of the gospel, but Timothy was not to countenance "fables," which II Peter 1:16 describes as "cunningly devised," and "endless genealogies." Both of these create questions rather than "godly edifying." Since God is not the author of confusion, avoiding these disruptive teachings is important. "Fables" comes from *muthos,* meaning "myth." Here the word apparently refers to traditional supplements to the law, questionable stories or "old wives' fables" (I Timothy 4:7), and Jewish fabrications such as those found in the Talmud.

Extensive genealogies are useless in promoting spiritual growth today. Such registers were used to foster Jewish national and religious pride. There is purpose in establishing the lineage of the Messiah, but otherwise genealogies do not serve a worthwhile purpose for born-again believers. "Edifying" here comes from *oikonomia,* which literally means "household economy." In God's economy, only those themes truly in harmony with apostolic doctrine should be emphasized.

Verse 5. "End" here means "the goal, the result, the completed product." The motivation and objective for these instructions is love. Putting down error and heresy is not considered to be less than love! Paul wanted both to show love and to evoke love—showing by correcting and evoking by suggesting to those engaged in Judaizing errors a better way.

Such correction is necessary in the body of Christ (II Timothy 3:16). It must be rooted in a "pure heart" (lacking improper motives), a "good conscience" (one without condemnation), and "faith unfeigned" (real faith without pretense or artificiality). We are to use the Word to motivate those in error to change their ways. Such usage in the right spirit constitutes love without dissimulation. (See Romans 12:9.)

Verse 6. From these things—a pure heart, good conscience, unfeigned faith—some had strayed, turning to worthless, unprofitable matter. "Vain jangling" is meaningless talk, semantic calisthenics designed to make one appear wise when in fact he is spiritually foolish. Perhaps it finds its widest usage in the pulpits and platforms of religion—although politics would follow close behind. The subject here, however, is religious teachers, those who wish to seem profound but are shallow.

Verse 7. These teachers appear to be the Judaizers, who insisted that all who claim Abraham in their lineage should keep the law of Moses. They enjoined converts to Christianity to be subject to the ceremonial aspects of the law. These puffed-up, proud pretenders did not know what they were talking about. They were yet blinded to the real meaning of the prophecies concerning the Messiah and the typology with which the law was rife. They were more in need of learning than of teaching others.

Verse 8. The law is "good," a fact that stands uncontested. But goodness is relative to purpose. A ten-year-old automobile may be a good car for a college student but quite inadequate for a traveling salesman. A man may be considered to be a good man, but by whose standards? Use the law, this verse says, but "use it lawfully," or in accordance with its true purpose.

The purpose of the law was to serve as a schoolmaster to bring us to Christ (Galatians 3:24-26). It cannot in itself produce true righteousness. It points the way to the Messiah through whom we can be counted righteous

(Galatians 2:20-21; Romans 10:1-4). To trust in the law to put us in right standing before God today would constitute improper use.

Verses 9-10. In Greek, the word "law" is used without the article in verse 9, indicating law in general. The passage apparently draws a comparison between civil law and the Mosaic law; thus, "a righteous man" here means one who is morally upright or law-abiding. The allusion to opposite qualities in the following clause further strengthens this conclusion. Law is enacted to restrain the ungodly, to curb their profanity.

The terrors of the law, however, whether civil or Mosaic, are not sufficient to spiritually regenerate the hearts of people spiritually. Love, grace, mercy, and forgiveness must come into play. They are incorporated in the new-birth experience, and they place the person under a higher law—the constraint of His love (II Corinthians 5:14). Jude implored his hearers to "keep yourselves in the love of God" (Jude 21). By so doing, we need not be fearful of condemnation by the law (Galatians 5:14; Romans 13:10). "There is therefore now no condemnation to them which are in Christ Jesus, who walk not after the flesh, but after the Spirit" (Romans 8:1).

Paul's identification of breakers of the moral law included the ungodly (*asebes,* destitute of reverential awe toward God), the unholy, the profane (*bebelos,* unsanctified, having no relationship to God), murderers, fornicators, defilers of themselves with men (*arsenokoites,* sodomite, homosexual), menstealers (*andrapodistes,* slave dealer, kidnapper), liars, and perjurers (*epiorkos,* one who swears falsely before authorities).

In the event Paul had not included some sin or class

of sinners, he denounced "any other thing" that would not be in harmony with sound doctrine.

Verse 11. Paul preached the foregoing message because sound doctrine was part and parcel of "the glorious gospel of the blessed God." He had been given a sacred trust—to know truth, to teach truth, to uphold truth.

Matthew Henry explained:

> Paul reckoned it a great honor put upon him, and a great favor done him, that this glorious gospel was committed to his trust; that is, the preaching of it, for the framing of it is not committed to any man or company of men in the world. The setting of the terms of salvation in the gospel of Christ is God's own work; but the publishing of it to the world is committed to the apostles and ministers.[3]

B. To Remember Paul's Personal Experience (1:12-17)

(12) And I thank Christ Jesus our Lord, who hath enabled me, for that he counted me faithful, putting me into the ministry; (13) who was before a blasphemer, and a persecutor, and injurious: but I obtained mercy, because I did it ignorantly in unbelief. (14) And the grace of our Lord was exceeding abundant with faith and love which is in Christ Jesus. (15) This is a faithful saying, and worthy of all acceptation, that Christ Jesus came into the world to save sinners; of whom I am chief. (16) Howbeit for this cause I obtained mercy, that in me first Jesus Christ might shew forth all longsuffering, for a pattern to them which

should hereafter believe on him to life everlasting. (17) Now unto the King eternal, immortal, invisible, the only wise God, be honour and glory for ever and ever. Amen.

Verse 12. Paul launched into a discussion of his own experience in the Lord, for which he was constantly grateful. The world is unthankful (II Timothy 3:2), but Paul entertained no such arrogance. He knew that he was a partaker of his position of service by the divine enablement of the Lord, not because of any virtue of his own.

Faithfulness is required of stewards with a trust (I Corinthians 4:1-2). Paul felt strongly that it was his duty to be faithful to his calling. Paul did not "handl[e] the word of God deceitfully" as false teachers did (II Corinthians 4:2).

Verse 13. Paul confessed that before his conversion he was a blasphemer (*blasphemos,* one who rails at, speaks reproachfully of). He directed his animosity at Jesus Christ (Acts 9:5). A Pharisee would not knowingly slander God, but Paul did not know Jesus was God. Mercy was extended because he "did it ignorantly in unbelief." Once a person comes to know personally who Jesus is and becomes a partaker of the divine nature by receiving the Holy Spirit, willful blasphemy and persistent rejection of God becomes an even more serious matter. (See Matthew 12:31-32; Hebrews 6:4-6.)

As a persecutor, Paul zealously tried to protect Judaism. He evidently felt that the end justified the means, clearing him to destroy Christianity. The word "injurious" (*hubristes*) reveals that his actions were insolent and violent. (See Acts 8:3.)

Galatians 1:15 seems to infer that from the start God

planned for Paul to do the work of an apostle. Such a purpose was not evident during the days of his attacks on the church, but in retrospect we can see that his educational opportunities and contacts readied him for this solemn responsibility.

Verse 14. Grace has no bounds! Regardless of what awful sins a person has committed, abundant grace is available from Christ: "Where sin abounded, grace did much more abound" (Romans 5:20).

But amazing grace was not alone—faith and love were a part of the package. The *Expositor's Bible Commentary* notes, "This is another of the Apostles' great trilogies. 'Grace' provided his salvation, 'faith' appropriated it, and 'love' applied it."[4]

Verse 15. "Faithful is the word" *(pistos ho logos)* was a phrase Paul employed five times. He added weight here by declaring the saying he introduced to be entirely worthy of our acceptance and full reliance. He was speaking of the fact that Christ came not merely to teach, or heal, or be an example, but to save sinners (Luke 19:10).

Paul readily acknowledged that he was "chief" of sinners. Such a confession was totally against his prior training as a Pharisee, but he was being transparent. We must be also, for who can say he has no sin? (See I John 1:8; Galatians 3:22.) Someone has said, "The beginning of greatness is to be little; it increases as we become less and is perfect when we become nothing."

Verse 16. When we are amazed that God does not strike out at gross sinners today, we must remember that Paul's experience stands out as an example of the virtually limitless patience of God. The word translated longsuffering *(makrothumia)* is "a patient holding out under trial, a long protracted restraint of the soul from yielding to passion, especially that of anger."[5]

The pattern (*hupotuposis*) of which Paul spoke is one that everyone of every age may emulate; the grace he experienced is available to all who "should hereafter believe." It is not God's will that any should be lost, but that everyone everywhere repent and believe the gospel (Mark 1:15; Acts 17:30; II Peter 3:9). And such faith leads to "life everlasting."

Verse 17. As he remembered the events surrounding his conversion, Paul erupted in spontaneous praise to "the only wise God." He referred to Jesus, calling Him "the King eternal," the absolute ruler of the ages. (See I Timothy 6:13-16.) He described him as immortal (*aphtartos*, not subject to corruption or death) and invisible. (See John 1:18; I Peter 1:8; II Corinthians 4:18; I John 4:12.) Some translations render "only" as "unique." Surely there is none like Him! (See Isaiah 46:9; I Chronicles 17:20; John 7:46; I Corinthians 8:4.) He is worthy of the honor and glory His redeemed people offer up to Him (Psalm 18:3; James 2:7; Revelation 4:11).

C. To Guard against Corruption of the Faith (1:18-20)

(18) This charge I commit unto thee, son Timothy, according to the prophecies which went before on thee, that thou by them mightest war a good warfare; (19) holding faith, and a good conscience; which some having put away concerning faith have made shipwreck: (20) of whom is Hymenaeus and Alexander; whom I have delivered unto Satan, that they may learn not to blaspheme.

Verse 18. Paul gave Timothy a commitment, or "deposit." It included the responsibility to warn Timothy and others away from dangers to their faith. Paul warned Timothy to avoid certain doctrines (I Timothy 4:1), false teachers and teachings (I Timothy 6:20-21), and particular individuals (II Timothy 2:17).

Concerning the prophecies mentioned by Paul, Vincent has provided this insight:

> The sense of the whole passage is: "I commit this charge unto thee in accordance with prophetic intimations which I formerly received concerning thee." According to I Tim 4:14, *prophecy* has previously designated Timothy as the recipient of a special spiritual gift; and the *prophecies* in our passage are the single expressions or detailed contents of the prophecy mentioned here.[6]

Paul used these prophecies as an encouragement for Timothy to "war a good warfare"—fight a good fight of faith. Warfare has its problems, its losses, and its wounds, but they are not worthy to be compared to the rewards of victory.

Verse 19. This verse speaks of "the faith" (Jude 3) rather than simply personal faith. (In Greek, the second occurrence of the word for faith is preceded by the definite article.) Holding the faith is the only antidote to spiritual shipwreck. The importance of a good conscience is emphasized by the use of the term six times in the Pastoral Epistles. The conscience can be cleared (Acts 24:16; Hebrews 9:14) or seared (I Timothy 4:2). Only confessing and forsaking sin can clear the conscience (I John 1:9).

Verse 20. Paul cited two examples of shipwrecked Christians: Hymenaeus and Alexander. These men are probably the coppersmith of II Timothy 4:14 and the heretical teacher of II Timothy 2:17.

"Delivered unto Satan" is probably synonymous with the action of I Corinthians 5:3-5. It involved excommunication from the visible body of Christ, which means the person was put under the hand of Satan. In some cases it may have resulted in physical problems, as I Corinthians 5:5 implies. The ultimate purpose of the judgment was remedy rather than punishment, as the word "learn" (*paideno*) indicates. Should they learn not to blaspheme, they could be restored. The verb translated "have delivered" is in the perfect tense, expressing that these two men were under the sentence of excommunication at the time of Paul's letters.

Footnotes

[1]Kenneth S. Wuest, *The Pastoral Epistles in the Greek New Testament* (Grand Rapids: Williams B. Eerdmans, 1954), 22-23.

[2]David K. Bernard, *The Oneness of God* (Hazelwood, Mo.: Word Aflame Press, 1983), 208-9.

[3]Matthew Henry, *Commentary on the Whole Bible* (Old Tappan, N.J.: Fleming H. Revell, n.d.), 6:808.

[4]*The Expositors Bible Commentary,* ed. Frank Gaebelein (Grand Rapids: Zondervan, 1978), 2:354.

[5]Wuest, 36.

[6]Marvin R. Vincent, *Word Studies in the New Testament* (McLean, Va.: Mac Donald Publishing Company), 4:214.

I TIMOTHY
Chapter Two

III. General Exhortations (2:1-15)

A. To Pray for Others (2:1-8)

(1) I exhort therefore, that, first of all, supplications, prayers, intercessions, and giving of thanks, be made for all men; (2) for kings, and for all that are in authority; that we may lead a quiet and peaceable life in all godliness and honesty. (3) For this is good and acceptable in the sight of God our Saviour; (4) who will have all men to be saved, and to come unto the knowledge of the truth. (5) For there is one God, and one mediator between God and men, the man Christ Jesus; (6) who gave himself a ransom for all, to be testified in due time. (7) Whereunto I am ordained a preacher, and an apostle, (I speak the truth in Christ, and lie not;) a teacher of the Gentiles in faith and verity. (8) I will therefore that men pray every where, lifting up holy hands, without wrath and doubting.

Verse 1. This exhortation seems to be an outgrowth of the charge in 1:18. "First of all" indicates something of prime importance. Public worship is the theme of the continuing discourse, and the primacy of prayer in that worship is the prologue of the exhortation.

Four of the seven Greek nouns used for prayer in the New Testament occur in this verse. The first, *deeseis,* is utilized nineteen times and appears here as "supplications." It refers primarily to petitions for one's personal needs and desires. We are to bring our requests to God in prayer (Philippians 1:4; 4:6). "Intercessions" (*enteuxis*) as used here has overtones of conversational prayer—a dialogue between friends—rather than a pleading on another's behalf. The word *entugchano,* translated in Romans 8:26 as "maketh intercession," implies "to intervene or interfere." This word carries the idea of coming boldly into the presence of the Lord as expressed in Hebrews 4:16. "Thanksgiving" (*eucharistia*), the expression of gratitude, should be an integral part of every prayer.

Verse 2. These prayers are to be made for "all men," but this verse emphasizes a certain class: "for kings, and for all that are in authority." The Christian has a responsibility to the civil authorities under whose rule he lives (Romans 13:1-7). One aspect of that responsibility is to pray for civic leaders. The objective of prayer for political leaders is specifically that we might live in peace, conducting our lives according to our Christian convictions and consciences.

Verse 3. The demonstrative pronoun "this" (*houto*) refers to the command to pray for everyone rather than the resultant conditions in verse 2. We pray for these people because it is right and proper to do so.

It is interesting to note that again the apostle expressed his clear understanding of the deity of Jesus Christ. He used the term "Saviour" thirteen times in his epistles, and the other New Testament writers included it in nine other verses. In six of those instances, the Savior is identified as "God our Saviour" (e.g., Titus 2:10; Jude 25). Paul referred to "the Lord Jesus Christ our Saviour" in Titus 1:4, and Peter closed his second epistle with a reference to "our Lord and Saviour Jesus Christ" (II Peter 3:18).

Jehovah declared in Isaiah 43:3, 11, "For I am the LORD thy God, the Holy One of Israel, thy Saviour. . . . I, even I, am the LORD; and beside me there is no saviour." If there is only one Savior, and if He is Jehovah, then how could Christ also be the Savior unless they are one and the same? The Lord Jehovah of the Old Testament is Jesus Christ of the New Testament! The name "Jesus" means "Jehovah has become my salvation."

As I Timothy 3:16 explains, "And without controversy great is the mystery of godliness: God was manifest in the flesh, justified in the Spirit, seen of angels, preached unto the Gentiles, believed on in the world, received up into glory." The Incarnation was simply the Spirit of God taking on visible humanity in order to fulfill the role of Savior and Messiah. There are not two Gods, two Spirits, or two persons in the Godhead, but one God (Ephesians 4:4-6) who manifested Himself in the flesh, in the Son, to redeem us from our sins.

Verse 4. God is "not willing that any should perish, but that all should come to repentance" (II Peter 3:9). Christ willed to save every person in every generation. The Jews received the new-birth experience on Pentecost, the birthday of the church, in Acts 2. The Samaritans (part Jew, part Gentile) received the gospel in Acts 8, and the Gentiles in Acts 10, thus partially fulfilling the prophecy of Joel 2:28-29. No one is left without opportunity to hear, know, believe, and be saved—regardless of age, sex, nationality, race, or social standing. God will not violate the will of any person by forcing him to accept salvation, but He offers it freely, without money and without price (Isaiah 55:1; Revelation 22:17).

Verse 5. In order to expand on "the knowledge of the truth," this passage again focuses on the oneness of God: "For there is one God." Jesus said plainly in John 4:24 that "God is a Spirit." The Godhead does not consist of three "persons" or three spirits. The one "person" of God is the Father/Spirit who came into the world as Jesus Christ.

Jesus was in very nature God, and He also had the nature of men. "To wit, that God was in Christ, reconciling the world unto himself" (II Corinthians 5:19). Thus He was uniquely qualified to be our "mediator" (*mesites,* one who intervenes between two, either in order to make or restore peace and friendship, or to form a compact or ratify a covenant). In order to mediate successfully and objectively between two parties one must share the nature of both. A man could not mediate between a horse and a man, for he does not have the nature of them both. The man Christ Jesus, being both divine and human, could serve in an exclusive mediatorial capacity. He positioned Himself on Calvary between the judgment of God and sinful humanity, and for all who believe and obey, He restrains that judgment (I Peter 2:24; II Corinthians 5:21; John 1:29; 3:16).

Verse 6. Christ gave Himself. What a superior depiction of the Savior, in contrast to someone who might have died with a struggle! Humans did not have the power to take His life without His consent (John 10:17-18).

The word "ransom" is *antilutron,* which was often used to describe the substitute price of redemption for a slave or prisoner. Wuest elaborated:

> *Antilutron* is a payment given instead of the slave or prisoner, that is, in substitution for the slave or prisoner. The person holding the slave or prisoner is satisfied with the payment as a substitute for the slave he owns or the prisoner he holds. The preposition "for" is *huper,* "for the sake of, in behalf of, instead of." It is used in Titus 2:14, "He gave Himself in behalf of us," also in Galatians 3:13, "Christ redeemed us from the curse of the law, having become a curse instead of (*huper*) us."[1]

The latter phrase of the verse—to be testified in due time— identifies the time frame in which the gospel of salvation by faith in the substitutionary death of Christ is preached.

Verse 7. Paul reiterated his calling, appointment, and ordination as a preacher of the gospel of reconciliation through Christ, especially to the Gentiles. His apostolic status had been duly defended in II Corinthians 11. He seemed to be sensitive about any question as to the authenticity of his apostleship to the Gentiles—"I speak the truth in Christ, and lie not." He spoke of his execution of apostolic duties as being performed "in faith and verity"—sincerely and out in the open where all could see.

Verse 8. Paul resumed his discussion of public worship and prayer with an injunction especially for men. The word "man" is *aner,* which is specifically the male gender, rather than *anthropos,* mankind in general. The verse does not express exclusivity in the matter of prayer, but it specifies that men ought to take the lead in public prayer and maintain a life worthy of such leadership ("lifting up holy hands"). They should not manifest a spirit of wrath (anger, ill will, resentment) toward anyone or entertain doubt in the heart. These are the general conditions for effective prayer.

Some versions render "doubting" (*dialogismos*) as "disputing," since it does carry the idea of skeptical questioning and criticism. "Everywhere" is literally "in every place" (*en panti tropoi*), meaning that such prayer should be made wherever Christians congregate to worship.

B. For the Woman to Serve with Meekness and Submission (2:9-15)

(9) In like manner also, that women adorn themselves in modest apparel, with shamefacedness and sobriety; not with broided hair, or gold, or pearls, or costly array; (10) but (which becometh women professing godliness) with good works. (11) Let the woman learn in silence with all subjection. (12) But I suffer not a woman to teach, nor to usurp authority over the man, but to be in silence. (13) For Adam was first formed, then Eve. (14) And Adam was not deceived, but the woman being deceived was in the transgression. (15) Notwithstanding she shall be saved in childbearing, if they continue in faith and charity and holiness with sobriety.

Verses 9-10. These verses provide instructions for Christian women relative to propriety and ornamentation. The principles apply to all of God's people, for all are to be "a chosen generation, a royal priesthood, an holy nation, a peculiar people. . . . strangers and pilgrims [and, as such, should] abstain from fleshly lusts, which war against the soul" (I Peter 2:9, 11). I Peter 3:3-5 likewise admonishes Christian women about the issues of modesty and adornment: "Whose adorning let it not be that outward adorning of plaiting the hair, and of wearing of gold, or of putting on apparel; but let it be the hidden man of the heart, in that which is not corruptible, even the ornament of a meek and quiet spirit, which is in the sight of God of great price. For after this manner in the old time the holy women also, who trusted in God, adorned themselves, being in subjection unto their own husbands."

"Modest" comes from *kosmios,* which means "well-arranged, seemly, decently, orderly." The instruction to wear "modest apparel" dictates the absence of anything that would expose the body indecently, or that would call attention to itself or the wearer in a way that would reflect negatively on the "spirit of holiness." The words "with shamefacedness and sobriety" describe attitudes to guide the woman in her selection of modest apparel. This combination of words describes a blend of humility, respectful timidity, and self-control. Modesty quietens the emotions, while carelessness invites lust.

Verse 9 calls for the elimination of ornaments. Wearing ornamental jewelry or extravagant dress is opposed to the spirit of modesty and sobriety. Gold, pearls, and very expensive apparel are examples of things that are not suitable for Christians to wear. They are not conducive to the Christian walk, which has as its ensign "separation from the world" (John 15:19; Romans 12:2; I Corinthians 2:12; II Corinthians 6:17; James 4:4; I John

2:15-17). Gold is an example of precious metal and pearls are an example of precious jewels, neither of which should be used for personal ornamentation. Makeup also violates the principles of modesty, sobriety, shamefacedness, and nonadornment expressed here.

In Paul's day, as in our own, prostitutes used ornaments to attract attention to themselves, and proud, self-centered persons used them to display their wealth and "liberation." These things have no place in the Christian's wardrobe. Conduct, not ostentatious clothes, is the means by which godly women express their faith.

"Broided hair" is one word in Greek: *plegma*. It means something woven or braided. While hair is not mentioned in the original text, it seems to be implied when compared to I Peter 3:3, which uses *emploke,* defined by Vine as "intertwining the hair in ornament." It seems that this phrase teaches women not to weave ornaments into their hair, such as strands of golden cord, rather than condemning the practice of twisting the hair together with itself for easier management. Hiebert comments:

> The common feminine tendency to extravagant personal adornment was so strong in Paul's day that he felt it necessary to add a specific reference to it. The reference is to "the custom then prevalent in fashionable life, of interweaving in the hair gold, silver, pearls, causing it to flash brilliantly in the light" (Harvey). All excesses of personal adornment which are opposed to the orderliness and simplicity of communion with God are in view in Paul's prohibition. He would exclude all that might distract the worshiper or reflect upon the

spiritual dignity of the members. The caution is much needed today.[2]

The New International Version renders verses 9-10 as follows: "I also want women to dress modestly, with decency and propriety, not with braided hair, or gold or pearls or expensive clothes, but with good deeds, appropriate for women who profess to worship God."

Verse 11. This verse and the one that follows continue the discussion of the conduct of women in the church. The term "in silence" (*en hesuchia*) simply means "quietness and tranquility arising from within." Women and men have the same spiritual standing in Christ, but in the administration of the church, male leaders are to have ultimate responsibility and authority The woman is to "learn in silence." Paul elsewhere wrote, "If they [women] will learn any thing, let them ask their husbands at home: for it is a shame for women to speak in the church" (I Corinthians 14:35). The context shows that the term "silence" does not prohibit women from praying or prophesying in church (I Corinthians 11:5; 14:31). (See also Acts 2:17; 12:12).

"With all subjection" denotes a woman's attitude toward church authority. In I Corinthians 14:33-34 the same Greek word is translated "obedience." In case some would perceive his words to be motivated by personal bias or prejudice, Paul stated that this direction was from the Lord: "If any man think himself to be a prophet, or spiritual, let him acknowledge that the things that I write unto you are the commandments of the Lord" (I Corinthians 14:37).

Verse 12. Paul did not allow a woman to "teach" or

teaching seems to be one of authoritative doctrinal instruction, particularly authoritative teaching of men. Elsewhere we find examples of women teaching children and other women (II Timothy 1:5; Titus 2:3-4).

To "usurp authority" *(authentein)* means "to exercise authority or dominion over." Some render the phrase as "to have authority over a man" (NIV) or "dictate to men" (Moffat). The use of the term *aner* (the male gender) without the definite article seems to annul the idea that Paul had only a woman's husband in mind. The context is the order of work and worship in the church.

Many Bible scholars explain this passage to exclude women from the position of preacher or teacher in the church.[3] Others hold that if the privilege of preaching or teaching is conveyed by church authorities, then a woman would be acting under authority and no unlawful encroachment would be involved.

Verses 13-14. These verses give the reason for the position outlined in verses 11 and 12: the leadership of the male is based on the divine order of creation and the circumstances of the fall of humanity. I Corinthians 11:8-9 also mentions that the man was created first and then the woman was created for the man. Of course, as I Corinthians 11:11-12 explains, they are mutually dependent. Erdman commented, "This [order of creation] to the apostle's mind intimated a certain independence or priority or responsibility which places upon a husband some duties from which a wife should be relieved."[4]

Verse 14 recalls the circumstances of the Fall, noting that Adam was not deceived by the devil, but his wife was. She was last in creation, but first in transgression. Jamieson, Fausset, and Brown point out that "Eve was *deceived* by the serpent, [but] Adam was *persuaded* by his wife" (Genesis 3:13, 17).[5] Of course, both were guilty. In fact, Adam bore greater responsibility as the head of the race and because he willfully sinned even though he was not deceived about what he was doing. Thus it was Adam's sin that brought the whole race under sin (Romans 5:12-19).

The use of the compound Greek verb *exapatao* (totally or thoroughly deceive) reveals how completely Satan succeeded in deceiving Eve. By contrast the verse simply uses *apatao* to state that Adam was not "deceived." Because of this tendency to be deceived, cheated, or beguiled, and because Eve did sin first, she was placed under the authority of her husband, a pattern that God still requires in the New Testament church.

Verse 15. Women who abide by godly principles will be saved in childbearing. Several interpretations have been suggested for this verse.

1. Since the definite article is used with "childbearing" in Greek, it is a reference to Mary's giving birth to Christ, through whom salvation has come to the world.

2. Women will be kept safely through the ordeal of childbearing if they manifest faithfulness and sobriety.

3. Women will be saved in spite of the childbearing ordeal. Jamieson, Fausset, and Brown say:

> Through, or by, is often so used to express not the means of her salvation, but the circumstances *amidst* which she is placed. Thus I Corinthians 3:15, "He . . . shall be saved: yet so as by (lit. through, i.e. amidst) fire"; in spite of the fiery ordeal which he has necessarily to pass through, he shall

be saved. So here, "In spite of the trial of childbearing which she passes through (as her portion of the curse, Gen. 3:16, 'in sorrow shall thou bring forth children'), she shall be saved." Moreover I think it is implied indirectly that the very curse will be turned into a condition favorable to her salvation, by her faithfully performing her part in doing and suffering what God has assigned to her.[6]

Vine seems to have provided what may be the simplest explanation and one in keeping with the context: "By means of begetting children and so fulfilling the design appointed for her through acceptance of motherhood . . . she would be saved from becoming a prey to the social evils of the time and would take her part in the maintenance of the testimony of the local church."[7]

Perhaps God provided woman a measure of consolation following the remarks concerning her introduction of sin and her weaknesses. Women have purpose, inherent strengths, unique abilities, a complementary nature, and by the grace of God they will finally escape the curse and judgment placed upon in the beginning—"if they continue in faith and charity and holiness with sobriety."

Footnotes

[1]Wuest, 42, quoting Moulton and Milligan, *Vocabulary of the Greek New Testament*.

[2]D. Edmond Hiebert, *First Timothy* (Chicago Moody Press, 1957), 59.

[3]See ibid.; Charles R. Erdman, *The Pastoral Epistles of Paul* (Grand Rapids, Baker Book House, 1983), 41; R. C. H. Lenski, *The Interpretation of St. Paul's Epistles to the Colos-*

sians, to the Thessalonians, to Timothy, to Titus and to Philemon (Columbus, Oh.: Lutheran Book Concern, 1937).

[4]Erdman, 41.

[5]Jamieson, Fausset, and Brown, *The Bethany Parallel Commentary of the New Testament,* Minneapolis: Bethany House, 1983), 1232.

[6]Ibid.

[7]W. E. Vine, quoted in *The Expositor's Bible Commentary.*

I TIMOTHY
Chapter Three

IV. Divine Order for the Church and the Ministry (3:1-16)

A. Qualifications for Ministerial Leadership (3:1-7)

(1) This is a true saying, If a man desire the office of a bishop, he desireth a good work. (2) A bishop then must be blameless, the husband of one wife, vigilant, sober, of good behaviour, given to hospitality, apt to teach; (3) not given to wine, no striker, not greedy of filthy lucre; but patient, not a brawler, not covetous; (4) one that ruleth well his own house, having his children in subjection with all gravity; (5) (for if a man know not how to rule his own house, how shall he take care of the church of God?) (6) not a novice, lest being lifted up with pride he fall into the condemnation of the devil. (7) Moreover he must have a good report of them which are without; lest he fall into reproach and the snare of the devil.

Verse 1. To set one's heart on some special service in the kingdom of God is praiseworthy. It is not inherently wrong to desire an office that expedites the Christian cause, but it would be unethical to actively seek the office, especially through devious means. Such a driving ambi-

57

tion could be the expression of carnal pride rather than true consecration to God's service. A person should seek the work, not the honor. The office should find the man, not the man the office. This verse commends properly motivated aspiration to serve in a leadership capacity.

In a day when we are surrounded by.many religious organizations and ecclesiastical structures that use Bible designations such as overseer, bishop, presbyter, elder, and pastor, it is not easy to keep the local church in view when we hear these terms. But elaborate hierarchial structures did not exist in Paul's day. In Scripture the terms *overseer* and *bishop* designate the same person or office and come from the Greek *episkopos,* which literally means "look upon, as to care for" (Acts 1:20; 20:28; Philippians 1:1; I Timothy 3:2; Titus 1:7; I Peter 2:25). *Presbyteros* (elder) and *episkopos* (bishop) in Titus 1:5, 7 also seem to speak of the same office. Acts 20:17, 28 further indicate the interchangeability of these terms. Today the church uses these biblical offices with perhaps slightly differing ranges of responsibility and authority. The popular term "pastor" (*poimen,* a shepherd, one who tends flocks and herds) is used metaphorically only once in the New Testament (Ephesians 4:11). It seems to be the same service described in I Peter 5:1-2, which says the "elder" (*presbyteros*) is to "feed" (*poimaino,* tend like a shepherd) the flock of God under his care.

"A good work" (literally, an honorable work) means that the bishop's office is productive and fulfilling, carrying with it respect and responsibility.

Verse 2. Those who serve in positions of ministry with responsibility and authority are to conduct their affairs with the highest degree of integrity. Lest any feel that deportment and lifestyle are left totally to individual discretion or tastes, this passage submits a list of qualifications that those serving in ministerial roles should meet.

"Blameless" indicates that the overseer should be above reproach—not liable to serious justifiable criticism.

"The husband of one wife" means the bishop should commit himself to his wife for life. It does not mean he has to be married, for Paul himself was not, but that he can only have one companion. Some commentators interpret it merely to forbid polygamy, or having more than one wife at a time. Alford disagreed: "The objection to taking this meaning is, that the Apostle would hardly have specified that as a requisite for the episcopate or presbyterate, which we know to have been fulfilled by all the Christians whatever: no instance being adduced of polygamy being practiced in the Christian church, and no exhortations to abstain from it."[1] Erdman likewise stated:

> It can hardly refer to polygamy, for this would be tolerated in no church member, and need not be specified in the case of an officer; nor does it refer, probably, to remarriage after the death of a wife, as Paul encouraged second marriages, and a man whose first wife was dead might be in all reality, after a second marriage, "the husband of one wife." It is quite possible that the reference is to remarriage after divorce. Such an act might involve misunderstandings and suspicions from which a church officer should be free.[2]

Probably the most widely accepted interpretation is that the Christian leader is to be the husband of only one living woman, there being no biblical injunction against a widower remarrying.

"Vigilant" (*nephalios*) is best translated "temperate; sober in thought; circumspect," although of course a pastor must be watchful as he oversees the flock.

"Sober" means "self-controlled, or serious minded." Such an attribute is imperative in making sound judgments.

"Of good behaviour" is a free rendering of *kosmios,* translated "modest" in 2:9. The basic meaning is orderly, suggesting the idea of respectability, or being honorable.

Hospitality (*philoxenos*) is commanded here, as well as in Titus 1:8 and I Peter 4:9. It is literally translated "loving strangers." *The Expositor's Bible Commentary* observes:

> Christians traveling in the first century avoided the public inns with their pagan atmosphere and food that had already been offered to idols (cf. I Cor 8). So they would seek out a Christian home in which to stop for the night. A valuable by-product was that believers from widely scattered areas would get to know each other, thus cementing lines of fellowship. So hospitality was an important Christian virtue in that day.[3]

The pastor is to be "apt to teach"—not merely having a readiness to do so, but possessing the skillful ability to communicate truth effectively. He must be a student of the Word, He must also be aware of the needs of his constituents and meet those needs by the ministry of the Word.

Verse 3. No one can be a spiritual example and a winebibber at the same time. Both Scripture and abundant examples show that, regardless of the conditions in the first century, Christians in general and Christian leaders in particular should abstain totally from intoxicating beverages.

A "striker" is one who loses control of his temper to the point of lashing out in physical force; a pugnacious, quarrelsome person.

"Greedy of filthy lucre" means "desirous of base gain." Adam Clarke characterizes this person as "using base and unjustifiable methods to raise and increase his revenues, trading or trafficking; for what would be honorable in a secular character would be base and dishonorable in a bishop."[4] Such a weakness could tempt him to misappropriate church funds or take up a means of livelihood that may be less than proper.

The Greek word *epieikes*, translated "patient," carries multiple meanings including being kind, considerate, gracious, genial, and magnanimous.

A "brawler" (*amachos*) is one who is a fighter, a combatant, contentious. The bishop must not be quarrelsome.

The bishop should not be covetous, literally "not a lover of money" (*aphilargyros*). Such love is the root of all evil (I Timothy 6:10). (See also Matthew 6:22, 24; Luke 16:13; I Timothy 6:6-11; Proverbs 15:27.)

Verse 4. The bishop is to rule his own house well. Loving, compassionate leadership rather than dominating dictatorship is what the Bible teaches (Ephesians 6:4; Colossians 3:19; I Peter 3:1, 7). To "rule" is to "preside over." The success of a leader's work in the ministry is often directly related to his success as a husband and a father. His children at home should be in submission to parental authority lest his sons in the faith turn out like his sons in the family.

They should be subject "with all gravity." "Gravity" is the same word translated "honesty" in I Timothy 2:2. A better rendering in this context may be "respect."

Verse 5. This verse asks a question that naturally follows the foregoing passage. The idea is that a man may not confidently guide the household of God if he cannot manage well his own household. The principles of godly government should be manifest in his home before he receives the responsibility of overseeing the church.

Verse 6. A "novice" (*neophutos,* newly planted) denotes someone who is a recent convert, or neophyte. A person without experience will likely make mistakes in matters that call for mature judgment. (See also 3:10; 5:22.) And such a person is more subject to pride after moments of success. The Greek term for "lifted up" is *tuphoo,* meaning "to raise a smoke, smoulder," and it conjures up the idea of "a beclouded or stupid state of mind as the result of pride" (Wuest). He knows not but knows not that he knows not! Weymouth translates this line: "For fear he should be blinded with pride."

The condemnation of the devil is a result of pride; therefore the neophyte's pride will place him under the same sentence. For this reason, we must be careful when selecting people to fill offices of responsibility. Quick elevation of a novice to prominence may be too much for him to handle.

Verse 7. Those outside the church deserve a model of the Christian lifestyle. A little verse says, "Two things I've had in life that's ample: good advice and bad example." Regardless of how well a minister is respected among his own company, relationships with outsiders must make a positive impact or the evangelistic efforts of the church will be hindered. Satan is the accuser of the brethren (Revelation 12:10), and he will heap reproach upon those who offend, revealing every flaw to the world to destroy the testimony of God's servants. The man of God is obligated to care about His image in the community. An unconcerned attitude could reduce his character to the level of his reputation, thereby, as mentioned in verse 6, incurring the devil's reward for his own carelessness or hypocrisy.

B. Qualifications for Lay Leadership (3:8-12)

(8) Likewise must the deacons be grave, not doubletongued, not given to much wine, not greedy of filthy lucre; (9) holding the mystery of the faith in a pure conscience. (10) And let these also first be proved; then let them use the office of a deacon, being found blameless. (11) Even so must their wives be grave, not slanderers, sober, faithful in all things. (12) Let the deacons be the husbands of one wife, ruling their children and their own houses well.

Verse 8. The office of deacon as discussed here seems to be a distinct position in the church. The duties and responsibilities do not seem to be clearly defined. Many commentators see the men chosen to serve tables in Acts 6 as deacons.

"Deacon" comes from *diakonos,* "servant, attendant," which in turn comes from *dioko,* "hasten after," like a runner. In many churches today deacons roles are clear-cut and explicitly defined. They most often fulfill the responsibilities of helpers of the ministry as well as

63

the congregation. In some assemblies, their duties entail whatever designations the pastor outlines. In others they serve as a standing board, with their role spelled out in the church constitution. The deacons in Timothy's day are generally considered to have been ministerial assistants, with both spiritual and physical duties.

A full measure of gravity (*semnos,* dignity that invites reverence and respect) and sobriety must characterize the life of the deacons as well as the pastoral ministry. This verse gives some of the same requirements for these servants of the church as given earlier for the bishops: gravity, not given to wine, not greedy. Because it adds "not doubletongued" (*dilogos*) for the deacons does not mean this quality is not also required of the pastors. To be sincere tellers of the whole truth is an imperative, not saying one thing and meaning another, or not telling one person one thing and someone else another. In *Pilgrim's Progress,* John Bunyan referred to "the parson of our parish, Mr. Two-Tongues."

Verse 9. Deacons must hold the mystery of the faith in a pure conscience. Vincent describes "mystery" (*musterion*) as "truth which was kept hidden from the world until revealed at the appointed time, and which is a secret to ordinary eyes, but is made known by divine revelation."[5] The words "the faith" refer to the body of beliefs held by the Christian community as given by Christ and the apostles (Ephesians 2:20). Embracing the faith with a pure conscience is the meshing of faith with ethics. Only in the personal commitment and holiness of the believers is the faith safely preserved.

Verse 10. Again the Bible reiterates the requirement of proven leadership. "Let these also first be proved" is another way of saying, "Don't install a novice!" This verse does not refer to a probationary period but to an intensive inquiry into the character and worthiness of the individual. Once this is accomplished, then the person can be installed and serve with distinction in the office, having been found irreproachable.

Verse 11. The wife of a leader must meet certain qualifications also. Focusing on the omission of the possessive pronoun "their," some commentators maintain that this verse actually mentions a third class of officers in the church, not merely the "wives" of the overseers and deacons as in the KJV, NIV, and most other translations renders. The word used here is *gune,* which can mean women or wives, depending on the context. It seems perfectly natural, after mentioning two classes of church officers, to proceed with a word to their wives, who in fact do participate in their husbands' work in a supportive way and whose lives reflect directly on their reputation as officers. The context mentions wives, children, and home life (verses 4, 5, 12). In any case, these women are worthy of respect.

They also must be grave, not slanderers, sober, and faithful. The term "slanderers" is taken from *diabolos,* from which we get the word *devil.* Slanderers "devilishly accuse" innocent persons of wrongdoing. "Faithful in all things" is quite comprehensive. It expresses the awesome responsibility that rests upon the shoulders of leaders and their families. These character specifications correspond directly with many of those listed for the deacons themselves.

Verse 12. The passage returns to specific qualifications for church leaders, again citing the rule of "one wife." Like the overseers, the deacons must have their wives and children under subjection. Having unruly, undisciplined children is often a sign of moral compromise, or at least, a lack of courage in exercising loving, corrective discipline.

C. Rewards for Christian Service (3:13)

(13) For they that have used the office of a deacon well purchase to themselves a good degree, and great boldness in the faith which is in Christ Jesus.

Verse 13. The deacons who render selfless and dedicated service in the execution of their assigned duties are promised a high standing ("a good degree") both in the sight of the assembly and of God. They will also enjoy "great assurance," or as Weymouth translates it, "and acquire great boldness of speech in the faith that is in Jesus Christ." This boldness is the opposite of fear, reservation, or trepidation in witnessing for Christ. The deacons will be able to conscientiously uphold the faith.

D. Personal Insights for Timothy (3:14-16)

(14) These things write I unto thee, hoping to come unto thee shortly: (15) but if I tarry long, that thou mayest know how thou oughtest to behave thyself in the house of God, which is the church of the living God, the pillar and ground of the truth. (16) And without controversy great is the mystery of godliness: God was manifest in the flesh, justified in the Spirit, seen of angels, preached unto the Gentiles, believed on in the world, received up into glory.

Verses 14-15. Paul planned to visit Timothy before long but wanted him to be aware of some vital truths, so that if Paul was delayed Timothy could teach them to the saints. One important topic was the exercise of various ministries in the church: "how people ought to conduct themselves in God's household" (NIV). Verse 16 defines the "house of God" as the church, the buttress and bulwark of the truth, or as the Amplified Bible renders it, "the prop and support of the truth." The church is a "habitation of God through the Spirit" (Ephesians 2:22), and each individual member is metaphorically a living stone in the building that is His church (I Peter 2:5). Lock explained verse 16 well: "Each local church has in its power to support and strengthen the truth by its witness to the faith and by the lives of its members."[6]

Verse 16. Here is one of the most profound statements in the entire New Testament. "Without controversy" simply means "confessedly" (*homologoumenos*), or "without question." The "mystery of godliness" is the entire divine scheme of redemption that was embodied in Christ (Colossians 1:27).

"God was manifest [*phaneroo,* to make visible or known] in the flesh." In other words, Jesus Christ was the incarnation (enfleshment) of the one God who had revealed Himself to the Hebrew fathers, Abraham, Isaac, and Jacob (John 8:58). He was the Rock that followed the Israelites in the wilderness (I Corinthians 10:4). Virtually every title of God given in the Old Testament, such as Almighty, Shepherd, Judge, Savior, King, Redeemer, and Lord of Lords, is applied to Jesus in the New Testament. Since the Holy Spirit was the Father of Jesus (Matthew 1:20), after the flesh Jesus was the "begotten Son." The Bible contains no mention or concept of an "eternal Son" or a divine "trinity." Christ's disciples and the early church taught no such theory. They understood clearly, although the Incarnation will always be a mystery to the carnal mind, that the one God had made Himself known in the form of a man (the Son). (See Philippians 2:7-8; Hebrews 2:16; John 14:8-9; Matthew 1:23; Isaiah 9:6.)

There was no confusion created in the minds of early Christians when the Bible spoke of Christ as God. They knew that "God was in Christ, reconciling the world unto himself" (II Corinthians 5:19).

Modern versions replace "God" in this verse with "He." Even if someone follows this reading, it is clear that the antecedent of "He" is "God" in verse 15. It could not be "Son," as trinitarians often maintain, for "Son" refers to the humanity in whom God was manifested, and the term does not appear once in the entire epistle.

"Justified in the Spirit." Jesus was pronounced and proven justified (vindicated, endorsed) in and by the Spirit. Wuest made an interesting observation:

> The words "flesh" and "spirit" are set in opposition to one another. The former word refers to our Lord's life on earth as the Man Christ Jesus. The latter word refers to what He was in His preincarnate state as pure spirit, as Deity. . . . To simplify the matter further, let us say that the word "flesh" refers to His humanity, the word "spirit" to His deity. During His life on earth, His humanity was clearly seen, but His deity was usually hidden underneath the cloak of His humanity. Yet, at times, momentary flashes of His deity were seen, such as on the Mount of Transfiguration, on the occasion when the Father's voice from heaven said, "This is my

First Timothy

beloved Son, hear Him." It was seen by His
spotless and exalted character, by His works of love
and power, by His words of authority. All these
vindicated, proved, endorsed, pronounced Him for
what He was, Very God . . . manifest in human
flesh.[7]

"Seen of angels." All the crises of Jesus—the birth,
the baptism, the temptation, the agony, the resurrection,
and the ascension—were attended and witnessed by
heavenly beings.

"Preached unto the Gentiles." Jesus was Messiah to
the Jews but Savior to the whole world. "He came unto
his own, and his own received him not" (John 1:11).
Therefore He was heralded among the Gentiles (non-
Hebrew peoples), many of whom gladly received Him
(Romans 1:16; Acts 13:44-49).

"Believed on in the world." That anyone would
believe on Him, when the Jews denounced Him and the
Romans crucified Him, was, in itself, quite miraculous.
Nevertheless, people of all nationalities and persuasions
would become His disciples.

"Received up into glory." "Into" (en) here means
"in." As Vincent said, He was received "with attendant
circumstances of pomp or majesty, as we say of a victorious general."[8] For the ascension of Jesus, see Acts
1:9-11.

Footnotes
[1]Henry Alford, trans., *Greek Testament.*
[2]Charles R. Erdman, 44.
[3]*The Expositor's Bible Commentary,* 364.

[4]Adam Clarke, in *The Bethany Parallel Commentary*.
[5]Vincent, 4:234-35.
[6]Lock, 44.
[7]Wuest, 64.
[8]Vincent, 241-42.

I TIMOTHY
Chapter Four

V. Specific Advice to a Young Minister (4:1-16)

A. Concerning the Coming Apostasy (4:1-5)
(1) Now the Spirit speaketh expressly, that in the latter times some shall depart from the faith, giving heed to seducing spirits, and doctrines of devils; (2) speaking lies in hypocrisy; having their conscience seared with a hot iron; (3) forbidding to marry, and commanding to abstain from meats, which God hath created to be received with thanksgiving of them which believe and know the truth. (4) For every creature of God is good, and nothing to be refused, if it be received with thanksgiving: (5) for it is sanctified by the word of God and prayer.

Verse 1. The instructions and information to follow was something that "the Spirit" particularly wanted Paul to make plain. The Pastoral Epistles are replete with warnings of this sort.

God knew what lay ahead for the church, and through the Epistles He allowed it a glimpse into the future. The saints by this knowledge would be able to arm themselves against problems. To be forewarned is to be forearmed. Heresies are more easily identified if God's people know they are coming. And yet, even after such warnings, there would be some defections from the faith. Paul had told the Ephesian elders years before that "after my departing shall grievous wolves enter in among you, not sparing the flock. Also of your own selves shall men arise, speaking perverse things, to draw away disciples after them" (Acts 20:29-30).

The "latter times" refers to our own day but does not absolutely exclude the fading apostolic era. In fact, the spirit of such backsliding was already at work as Paul wrote, as was the "mystery of iniquity" (II Thessalonians 2:7; II Timothy 4:4). Enticement to turn people away would come from "seducing spirits" (*planos,* misleading, wandering, leading to error), evil spirits of error whose source and mentor is Satan (I John 4:1-6). "Doctrines of devils" are confusing, deceitful, demonic philosophies expressed through human agents. James wrote of "devilish" wisdom (James 3:15), and Paul wrote of Satan's "ministers" (II Corinthians 11:15).

Verse 2. The false teachers who will become channels for erroneous doctrines will be liars—pretentious, hypocritical persons who do not fear God. Their consciences will be so desensitized that truth will have no appeal to them. They will appear to be sincere Christian teachers but will reveal their true purpose through their inconsistent conduct (II Timothy 3:5).

Verse 3. The passage does not leave doubt as to the kinds of doctrines it means: "forbidding to marry, and commanding to abstain from meats." Similar traditions were taught by members of the ascetic Essene community of Qumran, who repudiated marriage except for the preservation of the race, and then only with strict guidelines. They also abstained totally from meat. Some time later, some of the Gnostics would also practice similar prohibitions.

The word "meat" can refer to any food. Today we view it as animal flesh, but to the KJV translators it meant solid food in general (Matthew 3:4; Luke 24:41; John 4:32-34; 6:27). The Greek word here has this meaning. In general, the New Testament forbids dietary prohibitions, because God has created food to be received (partaken of) by Christian believers with thanksgiving. By contrast, ascetics often establish patterns of self-denial for its own sake, instead of for a holy purpose. We should note, however, that the New Testament teaches against eating blood and eating food that we know has been offered to idols (Acts 15:29; I Corinthians 10:27-28) and issues warnings against alcoholic beverages (Ephesians 5:18; I Timothy 3:3).

Concerning the prohibition to marry, the New Testament does not countenance compulsory celibacy. Paul did appeal to certain Corinthians to consider celibacy in order to give themselves totally to God's service (I Corinthians 7:1, 7-8, 32-35, 39-40). He did not put it on a higher spiritual plane or command it but only encouraged it for the sake of unhindered service, particularly in unsettled times (I Corinthians 7:25-26). The false teaching opposed here promotes celibacy as an indication of spirituality, leading to disillusionment and confusion.

The Gnostics taught that all matter was evil; therefore many of them practiced asceticism on the ground that physical pleasure was sinful. Holiness was equated with self-punishment. The Shakers had their own brand of asceticism, which included celibacy, as do many orders of the Roman Catholic Church and the Eastern Orthodox Church. The writer of Hebrews makes it clear that "marriage is honorable in all, and the bed undefiled" (Hebrews 13:4).

Verses 4-5. While common sense should guide the Christian in his eating, God does not demand a certain diet. Whatever he eats he can sanctify by the Word of God and prayer. Food has no moral or immoral quality of itself (Romans 14:14-15). Christians can, through prayer and thanksgiving, partake of it without spiritual consequence (Acts 10:9-15). Examples of praying before meals occur throughout the Bible (I Samuel 9:13; Matthew 14:19; 15:36; Acts 27:35).

B. The Defense against Apostasy (4:6-11)

(6) If thou put the brethren in remembrance of these things, thou shalt be a good minister of Jesus Christ, nourished up in the words of faith and of good doctrine, whereunto thou hast attained. (7) But refuse profane and old wives' fables, and exercise thyself rather unto godliness. (8) For bodily exercise profiteth little; but godliness is profitable unto all things, having promise of the life that now is, and of that which is to come. (9) This is a faithful saying, and worthy of all acceptation. (10) For therefore we both labour and suffer reproach, because we trust in the living God, who is the Saviour of all men, specially of those that believe. (11) These things command and teach.

Verse 6. The faithful teacher will take the preceding instructions to heart and pass them on to "the brethren." No minister worth his salt will refuse to warn God's people of the winds of false doctrines. It may not always be the popular thing to do, but it is his duty. Being "nourished up in the words of faith and of good doctrine," Timothy could exercise his senses "to discern both good and evil" (Hebrews. 5:14) and pass such spiritual knowledge along to the church.

Verse 7. In contrast to sound words and good doctrine, Paul implored Timothy to reject meaningless trivia, regardless of how religious it sounded. There were many myths and fables promulgated by the Jewish theologians and pagan religionists, none of which were profitable to the Christian. Included in these are the ridiculous, legalistic "commandments of men" (Matthew 15:9). Jewish religious leaders of the day had prepared their own voluminous commentaries on the law and taught their own surmisings as though they were God's commandments. One need only peruse such writings contained in the Talmud to see why the warnings of both Jesus and Paul were entirely justified. Timothy was rather to employ his time in activities producing spiritual benefit, such as thinking on good things (Philippians 4:8), being zealous for good works (Titus 2:14), and praying without ceasing (I Thessalonians 5:17). Such spiritual endeavors would provide "exercise unto godliness."

Verse 8. Physical disciplines have limited value, but the pursuit of godliness is beneficial in every way, both now and for eternity. Erdman's comment here is particularly appropriate:

> The severity to the body advocated by false teachers was worse than useless; however, there is a kind of bodily discipline which may be a help to holiness, namely, the refusal to allow the appe-

tites to rule the will, the restraint and control exercised over the body by a sound mind and a pure heart. Such discipline, like all physical training, does have its benefits, but there is even a higher discipline of the spirit itself, which brings to man unlimited and abiding good: "for bodily exercise is profitable for a little; but godliness is profitable for all things, having promise of the life which now is, and of that which is to come." A consistent Christian walk does not necessarily forfeit the best things which the present life has to promise, and it is certain to issue in the higher joys of the life that is to come. In a certain real sense the Christian "makes the best of both worlds."[1]

Physical self-denial has its place in fasting (II Corinthians 11:27) and abstinence (I Corinthians 7:5), but it is not as beneficial as godliness and piety, for these are "profitable unto all things." The body, however trained or developed, dies, while the soul endures. All of life is not lived here in this earthly sphere; for the Christian there is a larger life waiting on the other side of death— a life purchased for us by the Lord Himself at Calvary.

Verse 9. The "faithful saying" is the statement in verse 8. As in 1:15 this phrase emphasizes the point. It is a worthy and wise pursuit to lift our eyes off the physical realm and concentrate on the living hope we have beyond this existence (I Peter 1:3).

Verse 10. The Bible does not say that living for God will be a bed of roses. Keeping our eyes and our mind fixed on things above (Colossians 3:2) while the temptations and trials of this present life swirl about us is "labour." The

Greek word *kopiao* here indicates an all-out effort, a straining, such as an athlete would produce in readying himself for a contest. The term "suffer reproach" continues the same theme; it is *agonizomai,* which describes action as if involved in an athletic struggle. Goodspeed renders the passage as "toil and struggle," and the NIV suggests "labor and strive."

The reason for this striving, this straining, is that we trust in the living God. It is this trust, or more literally, this abiding hope, that makes the struggle worthwhile. Whatever persecution or reproach that comes to the Christian is not to be compared with the glory that someday will be ours (Romans 8:18). The hope keeps us steady in the winds of adversity. We strain in training for spiritual warfare, we toil against the misunderstanding of others, we strive against the opposition of the world, we labor to keep ourselves in the love of God—all because the living God deserves our utmost devotion and service, and because we want to be found faithfully serving when He returns for His church.

God is "the Saviour of all men." This phrase does not teach universalism, the theory that all people will ultimately be saved regardless of their lack of faith, obedience, or relationship with Jesus Christ. While Christ potentially saved everyone by His sacrifice on Calvary, it is incumbent upon every individual to manifest personal trust in Him and obey the gospel revealed in the Scriptures. II Thessalonians 1:7-8 clearly states, "The Lord Jesus shall be revealed from heaven with his mighty angels, in flaming fire taking vengeance on them that know not God, and that obey not the gospel of our Lord Jesus Christ." He came to save the world, but He is "specially" the Savior of "those that believe."

Verse 11. Lest there be any timidity on the part of Timothy, Paul charged that he command and teach these truths, as opposed to the false doctrines of verse 3, to the saints. These truths are not merely optional suggestions; they are imperative principles to guide our lives.

C. Perseverance in Good Works (4:12-16)

(12) Let no man despise thy youth; but be thou an example of the believers, in word, in conversation, in charity, in spirit, in faith, in purity. (13) Till I come, give attendance to reading, to exhortation, to doctrine. (14) Neglect not the gift that is in thee, which was given thee by prophecy, with the laying on of the hands of the presbytery. (15) Meditate upon these things; give thyself wholly to them; that thy profiting may appear to all. (16) Take heed unto thyself, and unto the doctrine; continue in them: for in doing this thou shalt both save thyself, and them that hear thee.

Verse 12. Even though Timothy was probably above thirty-five years of age (Vincent put him at thirty-eight to forty, and others approximate that suggestion), he was young to the Ephesian elders. At least fifteen years had passed since he had joined Paul at Lystra (Acts 16:1-3), yet to handle the responsibilities with which the aging apostle now charged him he was indeed young. (In the Roman Empire, one was considered to be a "young man" until he was forty-five.) Timothy was to respect the elders with whom he worked and to conduct his affairs in such a way that they would hold him in high regard.

The preceding passage instructs the young elder to teach and command certain doctrines. If any factor would cause trepidation in fulfilling this admonition, it would be his youth. In essence, this verse says, "Don't let your youth intimidate you. Conduct your affairs, both spiritual and secular, in such a way that no one can say you could have handled it more wisely had you been older and more experienced."

By being an example of the believers, no one would have an opportunity to accuse him and thereby diminish his potential for ministry. The young minister is to maintain an exemplary model in *word*—here meaning his speech, both in public and in private; in *conversation*—his daily manner of life; in *charity*—genuine Christian love, the fruit of the Spirit; in *spirit*—the manifestation of his overall attitude and spiritual motivation; in *faith*—here and in Galatians 5:22 this word carries the connotation of faithfulness as well as trust in God; in *purity*—blameless in morals and motives.

Verse 13. In the interim preceding the visit of the apostle himself, Timothy was to perform the duties of reading, exhortation, and teaching. "Reading" probably includes the reading done in the public assemblies, although private study of the Scriptures is also indicated. Exhortation is inspirational encouragement, or application of the Word. Doctrine (*didaskalila*) in this context is the actual teaching, or explaining, of the Word. It is plain from this verse that pastors are to focus on the study and teaching of the Word of God (II Timothy 4:2; Acts 6:4). In other words, here is encouragement to practice expository preaching.

Verse 14. Paul reminded Timothy of his ministerial gifts so that he would consistently exercise them. The talents, abilities, and particular spiritual endowments a person has are not to be hidden under a bushel or buried in the earth (Matthew 5:15; 25:25). Timothy received his gift (*charisma*) through, and accompanied by, prophecy, and it was symbolized in the actual laying on of the elders' hands. This "ordination" was the recognition of the gift imparted by the Holy Spirit. Paul and Barnabas had a similar experience in Antioch (Acts 13:2-3).

The Greek word *presbyterion* occurs only three times in the New Testament, the other usages referring to the Jewish elders of the Sanhedrin council (Luke 22:66; Acts 22:5). Here it means the body of Christian elders at the place where Timothy was ordained.

Verse 15. The word *meletao,* translated "meditate," intimates more than merely thinking on these themes occasionally. Timothy was "to care for, attend to, and protect" those things. He was to "give himself wholly to them," throwing himself totally into the ministry. Such an abandon would demonstrate to others in the church under his leadership that he had been "profited" (advanced, furthered) by these things.

It would be very difficult for a minister to fulfill this verse of Scripture without submitting to the discipline of an intensive study and preparation program. Those who feel called to ministerial involvement should gladly set aside time for training in the Word, in speaking skills, in ethics, and in social graces. Paul later insisted that Timothy "study to shew [himself] approved unto God, a workman that needeth not to be ashamed, rightly dividing the word of truth" (II Timothy 2:15). "Study" here means "give diligence to," but it is obvious that the study of the Scriptures is included in "rightly dividing the word of truth." It is the Word that people are called to preach

(II Timothy 4:2). How can someone preach it and rightly divide it unless he takes time to "meditate upon these things" and give himself wholly to them?

Verse 16. The passage continues to emphasize that the minister is not to let anything or anyone distract him from the ministerial and doctrinal course outlined for him. This verse uses the term *epeche*, meaning "to hold upon, fasten attention on," to encourage him to keep his eyes on the goal so that he will not stray, either from his work or his doctrine. (See 4:1.) Such steadfastness would negate any tendency to give credence to doctrines of devils and seducing spirits. He would thereby be saved, or kept, from heresy, as would those he was teaching. Seldom do laymen stray off on their own into false doctrine; they are typically led into it by a mistaken, deluded ministry. If preachers will faithfully and consistently teach the truth, heresy will have no foothold within the body of Christ.

Footnote

[1]Erdman, 60.

I TIMOTHY
Chapter Five

VI. Official Work with Specific Groups (5:1-25)

A. Treatment of Various Segments of the Church (5:1-16)

(1) Rebuke not an elder, but entreat him as a father; and the younger men as brethren; (2) the elder women as mothers; the younger as sisters, with all purity. (3) Honour widows that are widows indeed. (4) But if any widow have children or nephews, let them learn first to show piety at home, and to requite their parents: for that is good and acceptable before God. (5) Now she that is a widow indeed, and desolate, trusteth in God, and continueth in supplications and prayers night and day. (6) But she that liveth in pleasure is dead while she liveth. (7) And these things give in charge, that they may be blameless. (8) But if any provide not for his own, and specially for those of his own house, he hath denied the faith, and is worse than an infidel. (9) Let not a widow be taken into the number under threescore years old, having been the wife of one man, (10) well reported of for good works; if she have brought up children, if she have lodged strangers, if she have washed the saints' feet, if she have relieved the afflicted, if she have diligently followed every good work. (11) But the younger

widows refuse; for when they have begun to wax wanton against Christ, they will marry; (12) having damnation, because they have cast off their first faith. (13) And withal they learn to be idle, wandering about from house to house; and not only idle, but tattlers also and busybodies, speaking things which they ought not. (14) I will therefore that the younger women marry, bear children, guide the house, give none occasion to the adversary to speak reproachfully. (15) For some are already turned aside after Satan. (16) If any man or woman that believeth have widows, let them relieve them, and let not the church be charged; that it may relieve them that are widows indeed.

Verses 1-2. The word "elder" in verse 1 designates an older man and not an office. The reference to older women in verse 2 substantiates this conclusion. Timothy was to refrain from verbally attacking (*epiplesso*, literally, strike hard upon) an older man in the congregation. The *Expositor's New Testament* says, "Respect for age must temper expression of reproof of an old man's misdemeanors."[1] Older persons were to be entreated (*parakaleo*, exhort, beseech) as "fathers and mothers," while the younger men and women were to be dealt with as "brothers and sisters." The respect of a family atmosphere was to prevail. "With all purity" disallows any indiscretion that might be prompted by such a relationship. Ministers must avoid the dangers of impropriety that can be fostered by close association.

Verse 3. The word "honour" (*timao*) means "to venerate and revere." It conveys the idea of properly appreciating the value of someone to the whole body, or to the cause. That term and the context indicate that financial support is due those who are so honored. But they are to be "widows indeed," or those who are absolutely without children or relations. Hiebert added, "The basic thought in the word 'widow' is that of loneliness. The word comes from an adjective meaning 'bereft' and speaks of her resultant loneliness as having been bereft of her husband. The added word 'indeed' places the emphasis upon those whose circumstances are characteristic of real [childless] widowhood."[2]

Vincent made the following observation about the identity of these widows:

> Paul alludes to widows in I Cor. 7:8, where he advises them against remarrying. They are mentioned as a class in Acts 6:1, in connection with the appointment of the seven and also in Acts 9:39, 41. From the very first, the church recognized its obligation to care for their support. A widow, in the East, was peculiarly desperate and helpless. In return for their maintenance, certain duties were required of them, such as the care of orphans, sick and prisoners.[3]

Verse 4. This is the only usage in the New Testament of the word *ekgona,* here translated "nephews." Virtually all lexicons render the word "grandchildren." If a widow has children or grandchildren they should assume the responsibility for her support. "Requite" (*apodidonai*) literally means "to give, return, or compensate." It carries the idea that children are to compensate their parents by being responsible for their care when required. God recognizes the responsibility of a family to care for its own—"that is good and acceptable before God."

Verse 5. The phrase "a widow indeed and desolate" (*monoomai*, left all alone) indicates that certain criteria should be met before she can become a ward of the church. She has no children or grandchildren who could provide for her maintenance. She trusts in God, meaning she demonstrates faithfulness as a Christian. She prays continuously, indicating that since she had endured hardships, she is sensitive to the needs of others and so intercedes for them regularly. The prayer ministry of such godly women has made the difference in many lives, churches, and ministries around the world. Such care and activity make the widows deserving of support from the church.

Verse 6. Any widow who lives luxuriously or a life of careless self-indulgence disqualifies herself from special consideration by the church. "Is dead" is a present participle indicating that while she is still physically alive, she is useless, or as good as dead, to both God and the church. Such a person is "dead weight" on the church and unworthy of its continuing care.

Verse 7. Paul encouraged Timothy to admonish the widows to be blameless—irreproachable—and therefore deserving of the attention and care of the assembly.

Verse 8. Widows who are faithful to God and meet the spiritual criteria are to be first cared for by their own, meaning the descendants referred to in verse 4. A believer who refuses to take care of his own family is worse than unbelievers, for even they recognize their obligation to their own. Such a one has, in effect, repudiated the law of love upon which the whole Christian faith stands.

Christianity is a meshing of faith and works. "What doth it profit, my brethren, though a man say he hath faith, and have not works? Can faith save him? If a brother or sister be naked, and destitute of daily food, and one of you say unto them, Depart in peace, be ye warmed and filled; notwithstanding ye give them not those things which are needful to the body; what doth it profit? Even so faith, if it hath not works, is dead, being alone" (James 2:14-17). The absence of works negates the testimony of our faith.

Verses 9-10. These verses continue with the spiritual qualifications for the church-supported widows, but verse 9 adds the dimension of age—she must be at least sixty years old. She must also have been the "wife of one man," or more precisely, married only once (not having divorced one husband to remarry another). Some interpret this statement simply as a prohibition of polygamy.

She must be known for "good works," which include the rearing of children. The modern feminist movement has downplayed the woman's role of homemaker as described Titus 2:4-5. But wives and mothers who are involved in workplace careers to the neglect of their duties at home violate a sacred principle. Wanton women who have no concern for the Christian faith have so influenced our generation through the media and the political processes that many godly women have unnecessarily left their homes and marched off to work, putting their small children in the care of others. Such action could be a surrender to the selfish, materialistic spirit of our day, perhaps fulfilling the prediction of 4:1—"giving heed to seducing spirits." The Scripture elevates the labor of the homemaker here by making it one of the qualifications for assistance.

She should also be hospitable ("lodged strangers") if

she is desirous of the hospitality of others now. Of course, she must have done so with propriety, so as not to seem morally careless or ethically naive.

"Washed the saints' feet" indicates further the hospitality afforded in her home. It was customary in the Middle East to provide a pan of water close by the door for this purpose. While this practice fits well with the context, the verse could also refer to having fellowship in the church as symbolized by faithful participation in the footwashing ordinance commanded by Jesus in John 13:5-15.

Relief of the "afflicted" (*thlibo,* to press) means that she did everything in her power to console and assist those who suffered from the pressures of life, such as the distressed, the oppressed.

While this verse could not name "every good work" here, it does mention these few. The point is, as Matthew Henry suggested, that "those who would find mercy when they are in distress must show mercy when they are in prosperity."

Verse 11. The "younger widows" are those under sixty years of age. They are not automatically the responsibility of the church. Presumably, they are still capable of working in some way to support themselves, and they have a better chance of remarriage. If the church supports them fully, they will have much idle time, which could lead to problems. They may "wax wanton" (*katastreniao*), meaning "to feel the impulses of sexual desire." Lock said that the real meaning here is "to grow physically restless and so restive against the limitations of Christian widowhood." Their natural drive may motivate them to remarry, setting aside their need for church assistance and ending the special service to the church that they apparently pledged as part of receiving that assistance. Remarrying in the faith is not sin (I Corinthians 7:39; I Timothy 5:14), but it is a reason that younger widows are not to be put on the roll of those receiving assistance from the church.

Verse 12. To the English translators of 1611, the word translated "damnation" did not necessarily carry the idea of some future punishment or doom. Probably a more modern and understandable rendering would be "condemnation." The Greek word simply means "judgment." This verse seems to mean that by remarrying, a widow who is supported by the church has cast off her first "faith" or "pledge" (solemn promise) to serve the church.

Some commentators understand this verse to refer to marriage outside the faith in rebellion against the plain admonitions in II Corinthians 6:14 and I Corinthians 7:39. Such a relationship could easily lead to the practices mentioned in verse 13 and thereby result in divine chastening. (See I Corinthians 11:30-32; Hebrews 12:4-11.)

Verse 13. The tendency of fully supported younger widows is toward idleness and toward becoming busybodies who wander from house to house gossiping about others.

Verses 14-15. Because of the possibilities mentioned in verses 11-13, Paul recommended that the younger widows marry (only in the Lord) rather than being supported by the church, which they might disappoint or disgrace by the listed practices.

At this point, their responsibilities will be the same as those of married Christian women in general. They are to "bear children, guide the house." The Creator designed women biologically and psychologically to bear children, and they have the primary responsibility to guide the household. In fulfilling this role, a woman pleases the Lord, complements her husband, and discovers it a rewarding experience. (See also Titus 2:4-5.) Confusion, frustration, and disillusionment result from a lack of commitment to scriptural patterns.

If Christian women follow biblical teachings, they will give no occasion for the enemy to accuse them and thereby bring a reproach upon themselves, the church, and the name of the Lord. Unfortunately, some women in the church have turned against these godly admonitions and against Christ Himself, and have reverted to a life of sin.

Verse 16. This verse summarizes the comments in verses 3-15. It simply reiterates that believers are to care for the widows in their family so they do not become the responsibility of the church. In this way, the assembly will be free to take care of those who are left alone without any family at all.

B. Honoring Elders (5:17-18)

(17) Let the elders that rule well be counted worthy of double honour, especially they who labour in the word and doctrine. (18) For the scripture saith, Thou shalt not muzzle the ox that treadeth out the corn. And, The labourer is worthy of his reward.

Verse 17. The topic now shifts from the care of widows to the subject of ruling elders. This verse speaks of "elders" in a different sense from verse 1. That verse spoke of an older person; here the reference is to elders who lead, or pastors. The titles of elder, pastor, shepherd, and overseer have the same basic connotation and are generally interchangeable. Qualifications for such leaders are given in 3:2-7, but now the discussion turns to (1) honoring elders, (2) protecting elders, (3) rebuking elders, and (4) selecting elders.

This verse deals with honoring elders. Such honor must be predicated upon knowing them: "Know them which labour among you" (I Thessalonians 5:12). Their lives should be transparent to all, their motives pure, their labor flowing from a sincere heart. Honor, first of all, includes submission to their authority, and obedience to them as spiritual leaders (Hebrews 13:7, 17), but the Greek word used here, *time,* has broader intimations. While it does mean respect and regard, it includes the thought of financial remuneration, just as "honour" in 5:3 involves monetary support. The root word appears in "honorarium"—something paid for certain services.

The Scripture does not say, "Pay them well," because it deals with motives. The Epistles often couch discussions about money in language only those with spiritual motives will discern: harvest, seed, services, aroma, gift, bounty, blessing, grace. Similarly, today we do not say, "Here's your money!" but instead, "We want to honor you with this gift." The ruling elder or pastor has the "right" to receive of the saints material things since he ministers to them spiritual things (I Corinthians 9:11). But Paul chose not to take remuneration from the Corinthians for personal reasons; perhaps there were many problems that he did not want to complicate by giving anyone an opportunity to criticize him for impure motives (II Corinthians 11:7-9).

"Double honour" means that the elders who lead well are to be compensated generously, amply, according to their position and ability. The reference is to elders who demonstrate particular excellence in leadership ability and teaching ability, not to a supposed distinction between "ruling" elders and "teaching" elders. I Timothy 4:6-16 lists some pertinent criteria to aid in such a determination. Perhaps this description includes factors such as clear thinking, ability to communicate well, sound judgment, and evenhanded administration.

While all elders can teach, apparently not all elders reach the mark of excellence worthy of double honor. The contrast is not between good elders and bad elders, but it is a matter of good and better. "Worthy" means they have earned the honor. The word used for "labour" (*koriontes*) is strong, indicating hard work to the point of fatigue and weariness. These elders arduously devote themselves to strenuous study and to ministerial tasks. The assumption is that some elders work harder than others in preaching and teaching and are more involved in leadership responsibilities. The man who models the ministry according to divine standards, who gives maximum effort, is the man who is worthy of double honor. At issue here is not talent but effort. Mediocrity springs from an unwillingness to make the effort, to pay the price.

Someone told Donald G. Barnhouse: "I'd give the world to be able to teach the Bible like you!" His terse reply: "That is exactly what it costs!" Oswald Chambers in his classic work, *Spiritual Leadership,* said, "No one need aspire to leadership in the work of God who is not prepared to pay a price greater than his contemporaries and colleagues are willing to pay. True leadership exacts a heavy toll on the whole man, and the more effective the leadership is, the higher the price to be paid."[4]

Verse 18. Men who are called of God will preach whether they are paid or not, but it is God's plan for them to live of their ministry (I Corinthians 9:7-11). To illustrate the point, this verse uses the figure of the ox treading out grain, citing Deuteronomy 25:4. The ox that pulls the stone or sled to crush the grain is allowed to eat as he goes. In other words, "if the ox provides food for you, you should provide his!" "Much increase is by the strength of the ox" (Proverbs 14:4). Just as it would be unjust to muzzle the ox, so it would be unfair to refuse to pay the preacher! We are to support the one who teaches us (Galatians 6:6).

This verse also quotes the words of Jesus in Luke 10:7: "The labourer is worthy of his hire." Significantly, it identifies these words as Scripture, showing that at this early date the church had already recognized Luke's Gospel as the inspired Word of God.

C. Discipline of Elders (5:19-21)

(19) Against an elder receive not an accusation, but before two or three witnesses. (20) Them that sin rebuke before all, that others also may fear. (21) I charge thee before God, and the Lord Jesus Christ, and the elect angels, that thou observe these things without preferring before one another, doing nothing by partiality.

Verse 19. This verse introduces the idea of protecting elders, or insuring their safe and just treatment. It is a sacred trust to be in the ministry, and a minister's effectiveness is based upon his integrity, his credibility, and his believability. If he can be discredited and his mouth effectively stopped, it would be a major victory for the enemies of the church. Rumors, innuendoes, half-truths and outright lies are often the ammunition fired at the minister. Should these be given a full hearing at every turn of the road, he could be worn down and discredited whether the charges were true or not. No doubt some believed that Jesus Himself was what some of the "religious" leaders called Him—"a winebibber," a glutton, and an associate of drunks, prostitutes, and Zealots.

Therefore, when someone comes with a formal accusation (*kategoria*) against an elder, the administrative overseer must make sure that at least one or two others will vouch for the veracity of the charges and the sincerity of the one making the charge. (See Deuteronomy 19:15.) This provision constitutes tremendous protection for the pastor. Those who have to investigate charges of wrongdoing would be kept busy by gossips if they had to research every rumor thoroughly. Moreover, when someone charges that another person has wronged him, Scripture requires that the accuser first meet the accused personally (Matthew 18:15), and then have a private conference with one or more additional persons present (Matthew 18:16). The third step, described here, is to bring the matter before the church (Matthew 18:17). If the personal meeting and the conference have failed to resolve the matter, the case then comes before the church leadership.

Verse 20. Should the process determine guilt on the part of an elder, then public rebuke becomes necessary. Trench described such rebuke (*elegcho*) as "effectual wielding of the victorious arms of the truth, as to bring him, if not always to a confession, yet at least to a conviction of his sin." Such public disclosure and rebuke would make other elders think again before committing a similar offence.

Verse 21. Because a fellow elder and peer is involved, there is doubtless pressure on the minister in charge to go easy in such a situation, but this verse reminds him that God and even the elect (holy, unfallen) angels are witnesses. Under no circumstances should the minister or church show favoritism for one person over another. Judgment in such matters must be impartial.

The Greek text clearly identified God with Jesus Christ here. There is only one definite article for God and Jesus and another definite article for the angels. A valid translation here is: "I charge thee before God, even the Lord Jesus Christ, and the elect angels," or "I charge thee before the God and Lord, Jesus Christ, and the elect angels." This verse cites both the omnipresent Spirit of God and the example of God incarnate. (See 6:13.) For another example of the same type of construction in Greek, see II Timothy 4:1.

D. Advice Concerning Ordination of Elders (5:22)

(22) Lay hands suddenly on no man, neither be partaker of other men's sins: keep thyself pure.

Verse 22 emphasizes the importance of ordaining only those who are worthy of the title of elder. Haste in placing men into the ministry who are too young or unproven can result in their failure (3:6, 10), thereby causing those who ordained them to share in the responsibility for their failings. If a man is closely examined before his ordination, it may save having to discipline him later. His appointment should be based on his positive qualifications, his record, and his character, rather than merely the absence of sin.

The warning about participation in such appointments is underscored by this sobering admonition: "Keep thyself pure." Not only does this phrase speak of carefulness in the ordination process, but perhaps the emphasis is on "thyself." While dealing with the moral character of others the leader is to keep himself honorable, upright, and beyond reproach.

E. Perspectives on Health and Sin (5:23-25)

(23) Drink no longer water, but use a little wine for thy stomach's sake and thine often infirmities. (24) Some men's sins are open beforehand, going before to judgment; and some men they follow after. (25) Likewise also the good works of some are manifest beforehand; and they that are otherwise cannot be hid.

Verse 23. Paul recommended that Timothy take advantage of the medicinal values of wine (*oinos,* used in the Septuagint for both fermented and unfermented grape juice). This statement in no way justifies a Christian's drinking of alcoholic beverages. As Barclay noted, Paul simply approved the use of wine when wine may be medicinally helpful. In our day of medical advances, wine is not of significant medical help, certainly not enough to make it worthwhile to jeopardize one's character, reputation, and example in the community. The best rule for Christians to follow is stated in I Corinthians 10:31: "Whether therefore ye eat, or drink, or whatsoever ye do, do all to the glory of God."

Verses 24-25. This difficult passage is likely a continuation of the warning in verse 22 to ordain only men who appear to be fully qualified, and perhaps it also relates to the discussion in verses 19-21 regarding the judgment of elders. *Prodelos* here means "clearly evident and known to all." Some sins are manifest and obviously precede the perpetrator to judgment, while others are not in evidence and will show up later—"following the offender to the bar of judgment and coming into view there" (Amplified Bible).

Likewise, some people's good works are quite evident at the present time, and they can be used to help qualify them for ministerial appointment. But certain poor character qualities may not show up for a while, only time and circumstances bringing full disclosure.

Footnotes

[1]Newport J. D. White, *Expositor's Greek Testament* (Grand Rapids: Eerdmans, 1970), 128.

[2]Hiebert, 91.

[3]Vincent, 257.

[4]Oswald Chambers, *Spiritual Leadership* (Chicago: Moody Press, 1967), 104.

I TIMOTHY
Chapter Six

VII. The Believer's Economic
Relationships (6:1-10)

A. Relationships of Slaves and Masters (6:1-2)

(1) Let as many servants as are under the yoke count their own masters worthy of all honour, that the name of God and his doctrine be not blasphemed. (2) And they that have believing masters, let them not despise them, because they are brethren; but rather do them service, because they are faithful and beloved, partakers of the benefit. These things teach and exhort.

Verse 1. As repulsive as owning another person is to us today, slavery was an established practice in Bible times. It is estimated that half the population of the Roman Empire in Paul's day consisted of slaves. Christ's mission as outlined in Luke 4:18 included "deliverance to the captives," but He did not interpret it as the immediate physical release of all those known to be slaves. Israel was under Roman rule at that time, but Jesus did not advocate violent overthrow of that domination. He was not a "revolutionary" in the modern sense of the word and never was a proponent of anarchy. While He did introduce principles of love and justice that brought about the abolition of slave ownership throughout most of the world, His primary earthly mission focused on the personal and spiritual liberation of those who accepted Him as the Messiah. Such deliverance could make someone a Christian and a full participant in the church even though he was a slave (*doulos*), as in the case of Onesimus. There were also examples of slaveowners who came into the church, as in the case of Philemon.

The merits or demerits of slavery are not the subject here, but rather the believer's behavior should he be in such bondage. The believing servants or slaves were to honor (*time,* reverence, give due consideration to) their pagan masters, rather than entertain hate or resentment. In this way, they would protect their Christian testimony. Vengeful action or outright rebellion would potentially "blaspheme" or slander the name of the Lord and His teaching. Christians are to honor those who have authority over them whether they are public officials (Romans 13:1-7), parents in the home (Ephesians 6:1), or employers on the job (Ephesians 6:5-7).

Verse 2. By the same token, should a Christian be in slavery to one who becomes a believer, he should maintain the same respect even though they are now spiritual peers. In fact, he should serve with even greater efficiency because his service now benefits another Christian. *The Expositor's New Testament* elaborates:

> A Christian slave would be more likely to presume on his newly acquired theory of liberty, equality, and fraternity in relation to a Christian master than in relation to one that was a heathen.

The position of a Christian master must have been a difficult one, distracted between the principles of a faith which he shared with his slave, and the laws of a social state which he felt were not wholly wrong.[1]

A number of commentators suggest that some of the slaves were pastors of churches to which the masters belonged.

While Christian ethics are fundamentally opposed to slavery, the church evidently did not demand that converts immediately free their slaves. Rather, the transforming power of the Holy Spirit caused converted masters to treat their slaves as brothers and respected employees, in sharp contrast to the typical behavior of unbelieving slaveowners, and ultimately led to the abolition of slavery in the church.

All people are equal in Christ, but they do not necessarily have equal status in society. Some may never have large holdings, or be leaders either in society or in the church. Any recognition or position in the church, however, must not be based on a person's wealth or denied because of his poverty (James 2:2-7).

These principles are to be taught and upheld as sound doctrine and included in the pattern of behavior in the house of God. (See 3:15.)

B. The Source of Worldly Values (6:3-5)

(3) If any man teach otherwise, and consent not to wholesome words, even the words of our Lord Jesus Christ, and to the doctrine which is according to godliness; (4) he is proud, knowing nothing, but doting about questions and

strifes of words, whereof cometh envy, strife, railings, evil surmisings, (5) perverse disputings of men of corrupt minds, and destitute of the truth, supposing that gain is godliness: from such withdraw thyself.

Verses 3-4. It seems that there are always some detractors who insist on saying, "Well, that is your opinion. I have my own convictions about that!" These verses make it abundantly plain that Paul wrote by inspiration and that his epistles were "commandments of the Lord" (I Corinthians 14:37). Therefore, if people teach doctrines that conflict with these pronouncements, their words are not "wholesome" (*hygiaino,* from which we get hygiene, healthy; in other places it is translated as "sound" [cf. 1:10]) and could lead to ungodliness.

Such a teacher typically exudes pride—"I know as much as Paul! He's not so smart!"—but in reality he "knows nothing." He knows not that he knows not. The word used for "proud" (*tuphoomai*) here is very appropriate; it comes from *tuphoo,* meaning "to raise a smoke, to wrap in a mist." In modern vernacular, these teachers are "in a fog!"

"Doting" (*noseo*) literally means "to be sick," as opposed to wholesome, and was used metaphorically in classical Greek to refer to mental illness. Thayer suggested it means "to be taken with such an interest in a thing as amounts to a disease, to have a morbid fondness for." One translator said of the false teacher described here: "His disease is intellectual curiosity about trifles."[2] "Strifes of words," or literally, "word battles," seem to be the hobby of some. The NASB translates this part of the verse: "He has a morbid interest in controversial questions and disputes about words." These word warriors gender strife, envy, railings (*blasphemia,* blasphemy, slander, insulting talk), evil surmisings, and a host of other spiritual maladies. "Evil surmisings" can be rendered "malicious suspicions" as to the honesty of those who differ from them.[3]

Verse 5. "Perverse disputings" (*diaparatribe*) conveys the idea of rubbing together, or friction. False teachers are a source of constant friction, being destitute of the truth. The use of the term "destitute" (*apostereo*) here seems to indicate that perhaps they once had the truth but have become bereft of it and have disinherited themselves. The end result of entertaining heresy is the corruption of the mind. In the case of many early Christians, it resulted in a return to Judaism (Galatians 1:6; 3:1-3; 4:9-11; Acts 15:1, 24). For many today it means backsliding into the lifestyle of their preconversion days, or reverting to a former, less biblical religious creed or persuasion.

Being robbed of truth usually involves a return to the bondage of materialism, lust, and spiritual error. A sure sign of people who have gone this way is their warped ideology concerning the Christian's relationship to material things. Such people can even allow their minds to become corrupted to the point of believing that godliness is a means of gain. Indeed, in our day we can see those who have made the ministry *porismos,* "a gainful trade." Contemporary advocates of the "prosperity gospel" may fall into this category. We are to remove ourselves from fellowship with those who teach these false doctrines.

C. Godliness with Contentment (6:6-10)

(6) But godliness with contentment is great gain. (7) For we brought nothing into this world, and it is certain we can carry nothing out. (8) And having food and raiment let us be therewith content. (9) But they that will be rich fall into temptation and a snare, and into many foolish and hurtful lusts, which drown men in destruction and perdition. (10) For the love of money is the root of all evil: which while some coveted after, they have erred from the faith, and pierced themselves through with many sorrows.

Verse 6. The Christian is to pursue "contentment" (*autarkeia*) rather than supposed prosperity. Things are transitory; contentment is abiding, regardless of possessions. Jesus taught us how to think about possessions: "Take heed, and beware of covetousness: for a man's life consisteth not in the abundance of the things which he possesseth" (Luke 12:15). Solomon learned that wealth and riches were not the path to fulfillment: "Do not wear yourself out to get rich; have the wisdom to show restraint. [Here is why:] Cast but a glance at riches and they are gone, for they will surely sprout wings and fly off to the sky like an eagle" (Proverbs 23:4-5, NIV). He also warned, "Whoever trusts in his riches will fall, but the righteous will thrive like a green leaf" (Proverbs 11:28, NIV).

In the course of life, if earthly things come our way we should use them and thank God for them but place no trust in them. Dependence on them will replace peace with worry and anxiety. Our security is in Christ, not our possessions: "Let your conversation [way of life] be without covetousness; and be content with such things as ye have: for he hath said, I will never leave thee, nor forsake thee" (Hebrews 13:5). Those who possess contentment regardless of their earthly circumstances are truly rich.

Verse 7. This present world is not our eternal home; it is locked in time and we are headed for eternity. We are merely passing through as strangers and pilgrims (Hebrews 11:13; I Peter 2:11). We brought nothing with us into the world and we can carry nothing out. As White put it, "Nothing the world can give is any addition to the man himself."[4] As one undertaker put it: "There are no pockets in a shroud." We use what comes into our hands to get us through life, and we leave the rest for those who remain. Such an understanding promotes contentment.

Verse 8. We should be content with the basic necessities of life and not strive greedily for more. This is the only use of *diatrophe* (food, literally, "means of subsistence") and *skepasma,* (raiment, literally, "covering") in the New Testament. These words have been used in other literature to express a broader meaning than intimated here. The former may be anything that nourishes and sustains, while the latter probably means "protection." Aristotle used *skepasma* to indicate a house. So the two terms taken together cover the basic necessities of life, or as we say today, "food, shelter, and clothing."

Verse 9. Those who try to become rich (not necessarily those who simply are rich) fall into temptation, a snare, and lusts. The word "will" (*boulomai*) is not merely an emotional fancy but a desire that comes from the reasoning faculties. This desire to be wealthy is not a passing notion but a calculated and planned procedure to become rich. Such plans may sometimes come to fruition, but they never lead to happiness and peace. They guide the unsuspecting souls into temptations, snares, and into many foolish and hurtful lusts, which lead to ruin and destruction. Money itself does not cause these problems, but the love for it does (verse 10).

Riches are neither good nor evil. Covetousness, greed, and the sacrificing of time, family, prayer, and church in the pursuit of money are the real culprits. Doubtless there are wealthy persons who love money less than some destitute individuals who think they cannot afford to tithe! The best attitude for the Christian to embrace is expressed in Proverbs 30:8-9: "Give me neither poverty nor riches, but give me only my daily bread. Otherwise, I may have too much and disown you and say, 'Who is the LORD?' Or I may become poor and steal, and so dishonor the name of my God" (NIV). Jesus picked up this theme in His model prayer in Matthew 6:11: "Give us this day our daily bread."

These foolish and hurtful lusts drown (*buthizo,* plunge, sink to the bottom) people in the depths of destruction (*olethros,* ruin, but not altogether spiritual ruin, for the word may also involve physical consequences) and perdition (*apoleia,* utter destruction). To neglect or ignore such a strong warning is to invite trouble of the most grievous sort.

Verse 10. The love of money is the root of all evil ("all kinds of evil," NIV). Greed and covetousness can undermine the spiritual foundation of people's lives so that virtually any wind of temptation will blow them away. A person may fall into sexual sin, but where are the compromises in his life that made him susceptible to such temptation? Usually one need look no further than right here. As one writer put it, "There is no kind of evil that the craving for wealth may not originate, once its roots become fairly planted in the soil of the heart."

Spiritual leadership has always been based in part on a person's attitude toward money. When Jethro suggested to Moses that he appoint representatives (captains, officials) to assist him in his responsibilities, one of the qualifications was that they hate covetousness (Exodus 18:21). Elders and Christian leaders are not to be "greedy of filthy lucre" (I Timothy 3:3, 8; Titus 1:7, 11; I Peter 5:2). Such appetites inevitably lead people away from the faith, ultimately bringing into their lives many sorrows and griefs.

VIII. A Final Charge (6:11-21)

A. Alternatives to Materialism (6:11-12)

(11) But thou, O man of God, flee these things; and follow after righteousness, godliness, faith, love, patience, meekness. (12) Fight the good fight of faith, lay hold on eternal life, whereunto thou art also called, and hast professed a good profession before many witnesses.

Verse 11. Paul admonished Timothy to deny any carnal appetites for money. To "flee these things" entails a constant running away from temptation. By contrast the minister is to invest his time in following after righteousness and the fruit of the Spirit. This instruction is in perfect harmony with the command of Jesus to "seek ye first the kingdom of God, and his righteousness; and all these things shall be added unto you" (Matthew 6:33).

"Righteousness" here is not imputed righteousness that believers have by faith (Romans 4:1-8), but personal and practical righteousness manifested by a separated lifestyle and sanctified attitudes (II Corinthians 6:14-18; Romans 12:1-2). It includes imitating the character of God and manifesting spiritual fruit as described in Galatians 5:22-23.

Verse 12. Fortified with the armor of righteousness, we are to fight the fight of faith. Jude 3 similarly admonishes us to "earnestly contend for the faith." The word used for "fight" in verse 12 (*agonizomai*) is an athletic term meaning "to engage in a contest."

Christian leaders have to fight spiritually to maintain the integrity of the gospel, protect the church from heresy, and hold onto personal faith through storms of doubt and times of testing. Upon winning the fight, they will be awarded "the prize of the high calling of God in Christ Jesus" (Philippians 3:14). Paul later declared, "I have fought a good fight, I have finished my course, I have kept the faith" (II Timothy 4:7). The encouragement in verse 12 to "fight the good fight" seems to stand in contrast to the evil fight to gain money and riches. We should fight for faith, not finances!

Christians are to lay hold on eternal life as opposed to temporary things. We are to set our affections on things above (Colossians 3:2), not on the fleeting elements of this world. We are called with a "holy calling" (II Timothy 1:9) and a "heavenly calling" (Hebrews 3:1). Emphasis on worldly pursuits is not fitting for someone with such an awesome appointment, because his testimony would be imperiled, and many "witnesses" to his profession of Christ are watching.

B. Adjuration of Paul (6:13-16)

(13) I give thee charge in the sight of God, who quick-eneth all things, and before Christ Jesus, who before Pontius Pilate witnessed a good confession; (14) that thou keep this commandment without spot, unrebukeable, until the appearing of our Lord Jesus Christ: (15) which in his times he shall shew, who is the blessed and only Potentate, the King of kings, and Lord of lords; (16) who only hath immortality, dwelling in the light which no man can approach unto; whom no man hath seen, nor can see: to whom be honour and power everlasting. Amen.

*Verses 13-14.*The apostle again underscored the seriousness of his words. (See 5:21.) God is a witness that Paul warned Timothy to observe these things faithfully. This verse invokes the omnipotent Spirit of God and also the sinless, obedient example of Jesus Christ, who was God incarnate.

"This commandment" may refer specifically to the command to "flee these things" (verse 11) or to "fight the good fight" (verse 12), but probably it refers to the entire epistle. We must not fall short in any point—"without spot, unrebukeable"—until the coming of Christ. The second coming of our Lord is a prime motivation for godly living (I John 3:2-3).

Also intimated here is that these standards of righteousness will be in force and expected of God's people throughout the age. The mores and standards of the society around us may change, but the demands of the gospel will be the same for every generation "until the appearing of our Lord Jesus Christ."

Verse 15. Many commentators tie the first part of this

verse with the previous one, making them say that "God will bring about [the appearing of our Lord Jesus Christ] in his own time" (NIV). It is certainly true that "of that day and hour knoweth no man, no, not the angels of heaven, but my Father only" (Matthew 24:36; Mark 13:32). The signs of His coming will alert Christians so that they are looking for Him, and it is unto them first that He will appear (Titus 2:13; Hebrews 9:28). He will catch away His church as described in I Thessalonians 4:15-17. The second aspect of the Lord's advent will feature a full revelation of the Messiah as He takes "vengeance on them that know not God, and that obey not the gospel of our Lord Jesus Christ" (II Thessalonians 1:8).

"In his times" may refer specifically to the scene described in II Thessalonians 1:8 or in general to the entire array of last-day events. These times will reveal who is really in charge of affairs on this earth! Jesus, as God incarnate, is the only Potentate—there is none beside Him (Isaiah 44:8, 24). When John was privileged to look into heaven, he saw one divine throne and One sitting on the throne (Revelation 4:2). The One on that throne is Jesus. (See Revelation 1:7-8, 17-18; 4:8; 22:3-4.) John used the same unique divine titles for Jesus that this verse uses: "King of kings, and Lord of lords" (Revelation 19:16).

Verse 16. This verse portrays Jehovah-Jesus as the almighty God. The Greek word for "only" speaks of uniqueness. There is none like Him. He alone has immortality (*athanasia,* deathlessness, being incapable of dying). (Anyone else who will share in immortal life will do so only by His power.) "Dwelling" is *oikeo,* "to be at home." The Lord is pictured here as being at home in unap-

110

proachable (*aprositos*) light. Perhaps this description refers back to the experience of Moses when God told him that no one could see His face (presence, glory) and live (Exodus 33:20).

Since God is a Spirit (John 4:24), He is invisible to the human eye (John 1:18; I John 4:12). No one can see the divine Spirit of Jesus, but Jesus is visible in the flesh. He is the express image of the invisible God (Hebrews 1:3; Colossians 1:15), manifesting God's righteousness, love, and wisdom to the world. God truly is invisible and unapproachable except through the person of Jesus Christ. In the days of the Tabernacle and the Temple only the high priest could approach the mercy seat and the shekinah glory of God behind the veil, and only then with the blood of a sacrifice. Now all are "made nigh by the blood of Christ" since His death on Calvary opened the veil (Matthew 27:51; Ephesians 2:13), and all have the right to approach God on the merits of Christ's atonement. As Augustis Toplady wrote in his famous hymn:

> *Rock of Ages, cleft for me; Let me hide myself in Thee;*
> *Let the water and the blood, From Thy wounded side*
>   *which flowed;*
> *Be for sin a double cure, Save from wrath and make*
>   *me pure.*
> *Could my tears forever flow, Could my zeal no languor*
>   *know,*
> *These for sin could not atone; Thou must save, and*
>   *Thou alone;*
> *In my hand no price I bring, Simply to Thy cross I*
>   *cling.*

111

C. Warn the Wealthy (6:17-19)

(17) Charge them that are rich in this world, that they be not highminded, nor trust in uncertain riches, but in the living God, who giveth us richly all things to enjoy; (18) that they do good, that they be rich in good works, ready to distribute, willing to communicate; (19) laying up in store for themselves a good foundation against the time to come, that they may lay hold on eternal life.

Verses 17-18. The "rich in this world" are those who have abundance of earthly goods and possessions as opposed to those who have little or nothing. It is possible to be poor in goods yet rich toward God or vice versa (Luke 12:21). The children of God know the riches of His grace (Ephesians 1:7) and have found in Him "all the treasures of wisdom and knowledge" (Colossians 2:3). True riches are not silver and gold but the good and perfect gifts that come down from the Father of lights (James 1:17), such as peace, hope, love, joy, grace, and a host of other assets that are a part of this "so great salvation" (Hebrews 2:3).

The Bible does not condemn the possession of money or things themselves, but if these things cause someone to be highminded (*hupselophroneo*, haughty, arrogant) then they will contribute to his downfall. Those who are wealthy should do good and be rich in good works. In particular, they should be "ready to distribute, willing to communicate," or willing to share what they have with those in need (Ephesians 4:28). They should not trust in riches but in the God who gives "richly all things to enjoy."

The Greek text means they should not "set their hope on the uncertainty of riches." Nothing in this life is more uncertain than riches. They can be in abundance one day and gone the next. I once pastored a man who was extremely wealthy, but he began to make high-risk investments and enter into partnerships that were opposed to biblical principles. I counseled with him about the matter but his attitude was, "You pastor the church and I'll run my business. Don't worry about me, I'll be all right!" But all the money in the world cannot keep a Christian afloat if he purposely violates the commandments of the Lord. Within one year, this man who had every creature comfort imaginable, and who prided himself in buying anything his wife even hinted at wanting, was broke, driving an old clunker, and his pastor was buying groceries to put on the table so his family could eat. He was humiliated, embarrassed, and confused, and he ultimately backslid. He had trusted in uncertain riches. Our security is in the Lord, not in our stock portfolio!

Verse 19. Earle noted that "laying up in store" is all one word in the Greek, *apothesaurizontas.* It comes from *thesauros,* which first meant "a treasury" and then "a treasure."[5] The idea here is that by giving generously, people will be "storing up for themselves the treasure of a good foundation for the future" (NASB). The old saying, "You can't take it with you" is still true, but what God gives us we can use for His cause and thereby reap eternal rewards. Jesus taught in Matthew 6:19-21: Do not store up (*thesaurizo*) for yourselves treasures (*thesauros*) on earth, for where your treasure (*thesauros*) is, there will your heart be also. Obeying this admonition helps assure that the believer will ultimately lay hold on eternal life.

D. Reject Worldly Philosophies (6:20-21a)

(20) O Timothy, keep that which is committed to thy trust, avoiding profane and vain babblings, and opposi- tions of science falsely so called: (21) which some profess- ing have erred concerning the faith. Grace be with thee. Amen.

Verse 20. Here is a heartfelt pleading from the apos- tle to "keep" (*phulasso*, guard, in the military sense) what has been committed to Timothy's trust. He appealed for faithfulness in Timothy's responsibilities as a steward (I Corinthians 4:2). Each person is responsible for the "gifts and calling" (Romans 11:29) that he has received from God. Every Christian is also charged with the obliga- tion to preserve and protect the integrity of the gospel (I Timothy 4:16).

In the course of carrying out this charge, the minister is to avoid (*ektrepo,* to shun or avoid association with) and ignore godless (profane), empty voices (*kenophonia,* here translated "vain babblings"), as well as false "science" (*gnosis,*knowledge). This last term as used by false teachers was a misnomer—"falsely so called" (*pseudo- noma,* falsely named).

The term probably refers to an incipient form of Gnosticism, which later became identified by the use of this word, *gnosis.* Vincent explained:

> [The Gnostics were] the most formidable enemy of the church of the second century. The Gnostics claimed a superior knowledge peculiar to an intellectual caste. According to them, it was by this philosophic insight, as opposed to faith, that

humanity was to be regenerated. Faith was suited only to the rude masses, the animal-men. The intellectual questions which occupied these teachers were two: to explain the work of creation, and to account for the existence of evil. Their ethical problem was how to develop the higher nature in the environment of matter which was essentially evil. In morals they ran to two opposite extremes— asceticism and licentiousness. Although Gnosticism as a distinct system did not reach its full development until about the middle of the second century, foreshadowings of it appear in the heresy at which Paul's Colossian letter was aimed. It is not strange if we find in the Pastoral Epistles allusions pointing to Gnostic errors.[6]

Verse 21a. Following after doctrinal error, even if it be labeled "revelation knowledge," leads only to the shipwreck of true faith. The intimation here is that an individual can corrupt or lose his personal faith as well as his place in "the faith." For this reason, believers are to separate themselves from those who are inebriated on worldly wisdom or sensationalism. Failure to do so causes one to "err" (*astocheo,* to miss the mark). To miss the mark of God's prize (Philippians 3:14) would be tragic indeed.

E. The Benediction (6:21b)
Verse 16. The benediction is fitting for a young elder—"Grace be with thee." The minister certainly needs grace in shepherding his flock. When the pressures mount and the problems come like a flood, it is comforting to

know that God's grace is sufficient (II Corinthians 12:9). Paul wanted Timothy to enjoy the same riches of His grace that he had inherited.

"Amen"—so be it in every life, in every church, in every generation.

Footnotes

[1]White, *Expositor's Greek Testament,* 140.
[2]Ibid., 141.
[3]Ibid., 142.
[4]Ibid., 143.
[5]Ralph Earle, *Word Meanings in the New Testament* (Grand Rapids: Baker Book House, 1986), 400.
[6]Vincent, 283-84.

THE SECOND EPISTLE OF PAUL THE APOSTLE TO

TIMOTHY

Introduction to
Second Timothy

The Author
The author of the epistle introduces himself as "Paul, an apostle of Jesus Christ." While some deny Paul's authorship because of the particular style of the Pastorals, conservative scholars accept that the apostle Paul was indeed the author. (See the General Introduction.)

The Recipient
The author addresses the letter "to Timothy, my dearly beloved son." He was Paul's protege, having been converted by the apostle and trained in ministry by him. At this point he was now approaching forty years of age and was a seasoned elder. His charge at the time was the church at Ephesus. He had been left there by Paul to oversee the work, which was being challenged by heretics and apostasy. An assignment of that magnitude deserved the helping hands of his spiritual mentor. It was a heavy responsibility and he no doubt deeply appreciated the continuing care and concern demonstrated by Paul.

Some say that Timothy was by nature timid and sensitive, perhaps plagued by self-doubts and a sense of inadequacy. If so, that may be the reason for the departure from the normal Pauline style to a more down-to-earth, pragmatic approach. There were enemies within and without, making eternal vigilance necessary for survival. The savage persecutions of Nero were approaching their apex, resulting in the death of thousands of Christians. The false teachers were at Timothy's heels, nipping like hounds at a rabbit. Nothing indicates that Timothy was not up to the task, however; evidently he was effective in the mission assigned to him.

Place and Date of Writing

Paul wrote from his prison cell in Rome. It is easy to imagine an aged, deserted man wasting away in a dark, damp dungeon. It may have been just like that, far different from his first Roman imprisonment, which amounted to merely house arrest. What is purported to have been his quarters in the Mamartine Prison are altogether undesirable. The food was let down to the prisoners there through a hole in the ceiling. Whatever the conditions, Paul was a prisoner of Nero, the mad emperor who had himself set on fire the Eternal City and blamed it on the Christians. And Nero was intent on getting his pound of flesh.

Paul's only companion was Luke. He may have been the one who actually recorded the moving farewell letter to Timothy in A.D. 66 or 67.

Emphasis and Style

The epistle seems to underscore three words: *endure, keep, preach.* The young elder was to *endure* "hardness"—tough times that would include the challenges of heresy within the church and persecution from without. He was to *keep* "that good thing" that the Holy Spirit

120

had committed unto him. He was to *preach* "the word." What was to be *protected* in I Timothy, was to be *proclaimed* in II Timothy.

Perhaps no biblical treatise equals this letter in the way it combines pragmatism and pathos. In a very personal style, defying rigid classification, Paul wrote his final correspondence from a Roman prison. Emotion seemed to flow from his heart through the pen. He knew he was going to die at the hands of the executioner soon, but it is not the emotion of fear that bleeds through. He was ready to die. Clearly, he was yet torn between a desire to depart (a euphemism for death in those times) and a desire to stay and continue his propagation and defense of the gospel. (See Philippians 1:20-25.) II Timothy could aptly be called Paul's Last Will and Testament.

Since he knew that he would be "departing" soon he admonished Timothy to pick up the torch of truth and carry on bravely. His strong adjuration in chapter 4 is one of the most quoted passages in the Bible. It provided Timothy with a certain sound, a clear direction. Thousands of gospel ministers since that time have heard the same charge read to them as they were inducted into the fellowship of the ordained.

Paul's last request was that Timothy leave his post in the care of another and come to his side. The comfort of Christian fellowship has no better illustration than the last written words of Paul.

Outline of Second Timothy

I. Salutation (1:1-2)

II. Paul's Gratitude (1:3-7)
    A. For Timothy's Friendship (1:3-4)
    B. For Timothy's Faith (1:5a)
    C. For Timothy's Heritage (1:5b)
    D. For Timothy's Gift (1:6-7)

III. Paul's Suffering (1:8-18)
    A. As a Prisoner (1:8)
    B. Unashamed in Suffering (1:9-12)
    C. Faithfulness in Suffering (1:13-14)
    D. As One Deserted (1:15)
    E. Aided by a Friend (1:16-18)

IV. Occupations of the Christian (2:1-26)
    A. A Steward (2:1-2)
    B. A Soldier (2:3-4)
    C. An Athlete (2:5)
    D. A Farmer (2:6-7)
    E. An Instructor (2:8-14)
    F. A Student (2:15-19)
    G. A Vessel (2:20-22)
    H. A Servant (2:23-26)

V. Enduring in the End Time (3:1-17)
   A. Perilous Times (3:1)
   B. The Temptations of Flesh and Spirit (3:2-5)
   C. False Religion (3:6-9)
   D. Persecution for the Faith (3:10-13)
   E. The Means to Overcome (3:14-17)

VI. Paul's Final Charge (4:1-5)
   A. Responsibility before God (4:1)
   B. Using the Word (4:2)
   C. Warning of Apostasy (4:3-4)
   D. Faithfulness in Ministry (4:5)

VII. Paul's Final Testimony (4:6-8)
   A. His Readiness To Depart This Life (4:6)
   B. His Record of Spiritual Accomplishments (4:7)
   C. His Anticipation of Eternal Life (4:8)

VIII. Paul's Final Instructions (4:9-15)
   A. For Timothy To Join Him in Rome (4:9-12)
   B. Bring Some Important Items (4:13)
   C. Beware of Alexander (4:14-15)

IX. Paul's Final Report (4:16-18)
   A. His Lonely Defense before the Roman Court (4:16)
   B. His Divine Counsel (4:17)
   C. His Confidence of Future Assistance (4:18)

X. Paul's Final Greetings and Farewell (4:19-22)
   A. Salutation to Friends (4:19)

B. Information about Friends (4:20)
C. Salutation from Friends (4:21)
D. Benediction (4:22)

II TIMOTHY
Chapter One

I. Salutation (1:1-2)
(1) Paul, an apostle of Jesus Christ by the will of God, according to the promise of life which is in Christ Jesus, (2) to Timothy, my dearly beloved son: Grace, mercy and peace, from God the Father and Christ Jesus our Lord.

Verse 1. Paul began five of his epistles with the same basic designation: "Paul, an apostle of Jesus Christ by the will of God. . . ." (See also I Corinthians, II Corinthians, Ephesians, Colossians.) It represents only a slight variation from his first letter to Timothy. Paul wished both to identify himself and reestablish his apostolic authority at the outset.

This is Paul's final letter and he made it clear that, even though the spectre of death loomed near, he yet had life—and that he recognized it as emanating from Christ. Paul lived life to the hilt. He found it exciting and fulfilling. He experienced all its joys without becoming haughty and all of its sorrows without becoming bitter. He had learned the value of contentment (Philippians 4:11-13). He had discovered that Christ has "given unto us all things that pertain unto life and godliness" (II Peter 1:3). Was it the divine appointment to apostleship that made life so full for him? Would he have been so vivacious had he filled a layman's shoes? Probably, because he knew how to give and take, ebb and flow—to bend without breaking, to understand while others endured confusion. All the dimensions of life seemed familiar to him.

Verse 2. His tender greeting is touching: "my dearly beloved [*agapetos*] son." It sets the stage for his very personal letter. He proceeded to pour out his heart to his true son in the faith (I Timothy 1:2). He was transparent, revealing what he felt most deeply about. He employed language that Timothy would easily understand as he discussed the themes so appropriate for a final message to a young preacher. He reminded Timothy of his spiritual roots, warned him of those who would subvert the gospel, and cautioned him about the attraction of wealth. For further discussion of the salutation, see the commentary on I Timothy 1:1-2.

II. Paul's Gratitude (1:3-7)

A. For Timothy's Friendship (1:3-4)

(3) I thank God, whom I serve from my forefathers with pure conscience, that without ceasing I have remembrance of thee in my prayers night and day; (4) greatly desiring to see thee, being mindful of thy tears, that I may be filled with joy.

Verses 3-4. Paul expressed thankfulness with reference to his memory of Timothy's tender spirit—"thy tears." Paul missed having his loyal friend by his side. He knew Timothy was a young man and was serving in the midst of critical elements that were poised to take advantage of his youth. His heart went out to him, and in his prayers he made Timothy a focal point. He wanted and needed him to succeed in his mission in Ephesus. He had been moved by his tears, probably shed when they had said their farewells. (See Acts 20:37.) The memory made Paul desire to see his young friend again before his death. He anticipated the joy he expected at a reunion.

The mention of a clear conscience indicates that Paul had discharged all his God-given responsibilities faithfully. (See Acts 20:27.) There was no condemnation in his heart, no skeletons in the closet, no major ongoing failings to hound him.

B. For Timothy's Faith (1:5a)
(5a) When I call to remembrance the unfeigned faith that is in thee.

Verse 5a. Also brought to Paul's mind was the sincere commitment of Timothy to the faith, which was handed down from his grandmother and mother. "Unfeigned" (*anupokritos*) is another way to say "sincere." Our word "hypocrite" is derived from the same Greek root. The prefix *a* negates its meaning, thus indicating "unhypocritical." Timothy's loyalty to "the faith" was an outward expression of his strong personal faith in Christ.

C. For Timothy's Heritage (1:5b)
Which dwelt first in thy grandmother Lois, and thy mother Eunice; and I am persuaded that in thee also.

Verse 5b. Timothy's spirit was the natural result of having been reared by a God-fearing mother and grand-

127

mother. Paul appreciated his own religious heritage—"from my forefathers" (verse 3)—and all who have enjoyed a Christian environment in their youth should. The inheritance of godly traditions and religious instincts is a valued possession. It is grounds for gratitude. The original faith of Lois and Eunice was not Christian but Jewish, but Christianity has it roots in Judaism. The God is the same. Jehovah, the Father God of the Old Testament, became Jesus, the Son of God, in the New Testament. The two religions were not totally distinct; but one grew out of the other, becoming its fulfillment and culmination.

D. For Timothy's Gift (1:6-7)

(6) Wherefore I put thee in remembrance that thou stir up the gift of God, which is in thee by the putting on of my hands. (7) For God hath not given us the spirit of fear; but of power, and of love, and of a sound mind.

Verse 6. "To stir up" is literally "to rekindle, to keep blazing." It does not imply that Timothy's zeal had grown cold; to "keep stirring up" is perhaps more accurate here. Anyone who has ever tended a fire knows that it needs frequent stirring, or renewing. The fire of our commitment demands occasional revitalizing also. Some of the same disciples who received the Holy Spirit on the Day of Pentecost were refilled in a later prayer meeting (Acts 2:4; 4:31).

The "gift of God" is not identified. *Charisma,* a gift emanating from the Holy Spirit, is the term used here. Some interpret it as a special grace, perhaps relating to administration, received by Timothy to equip him for his particular function in the church.

"By the putting on of my hands" probably refers to Timothy's ordination, although it is not explicitly identified. The event could possibly have happened in a public service or even in a private meeting of the two of them. More likely Paul was joined by the presbytery in this act when Timothy's qualifications were recognized as fitting him for the ministry (I Timothy 4:14).

Verse 7. God endows his people with the potential to be fearless in their service to Him and gives them the special strength, love, and self-discipline needed for spiritual achievement. "Sound mind," *sophronismos,* is generally translated "discipline, self-control."

III. Paul's Suffering(1:8-18)

A. As a Prisoner (1:8)
(8) Be not thou therefore ashamed of the testimony of our Lord, nor of me his prisoner: but be thou partaker of the afflictions of the gospel according to the power of God.

Verse 8. "Testimony" as used here means the ethical teachings and moral attitudes outlined by the Lord. There is never a justifiable reason to be ashamed of this testimony. Paul made it clear that he was not ashamed of the gospel of Christ (Romans 1:16). He did not suggest that Timothy was ashamed but used the Greek subjunctive, which here means "don't start."

Paul added himself in this admonition—"nor of me." Others had forsaken him (1:15; 4:10), evidently being ashamed of his bonds or his boldness, or fearing for themselves in the company of one who lived so dangerously. The appeal is for Timothy also to endure the afflic-

129

tions (hardships) that accompany the preaching of the gospel. (See Colossians 1:24.) For such endurance we can rely on "the power of God," for it is He "who hath saved us, and called us" (verse 9). The One who asks us to jeopardize our lives and reputations will not forsake us in the discharging of those duties. We are in His service and in His care.

B. Unashamed in Suffering (1:9-12)

(9) Who hath saved us, and called us with an holy calling, not according to our works, but according to his own purpose and grace, which was given us in Christ Jesus before the world began, (10) but is now made manifest by the appearing of our Saviour Jesus Christ, who hath abolished death, and hath brought life and immortality to light through the gospel: (11) whereunto I am appointed a preacher, and an apostle, and a teacher of the Gentiles. (12) For the which cause I also suffer these things; nevertheless I am not ashamed: for I know whom I have believed, and am persuaded that he is able to keep that which I have committed unto him against that day.

Verse 9. Our "holy calling," including salvation and service, does not come to us through our works, or because of our good deeds, but by and through the grace of God. God predestined for this grace to be granted to the church before the world began, or literally, "before eternal times." It was planned before any time frame conceivable by humans. Vincent said, "The gift planned and ordered in the eternal counsels is here treated as an actual bestowment."[1] This purpose and grace is now made manifest by the appearing of Jesus Christ. His birth, life, teachings, death, burial, and resurrection are all part of this "manifestation." The gospel reveals God's plan to give eternal life and immortality to every believer (Romans 1:16).

Verse 10. The abolition of death does not mean that Christians will never die physically, for indeed they do taste of physical death. Physical death, the most marked judgment resulting from the fall of humanity, is the last enemy that shall be destroyed by the immortality bought for us at Calvary (I Corinthians 15:26). This victory will take place by the resurrection.

Verse 11. This verse describes events transpiring because of "the gospel." Paul was appointed as a "preacher." The Greek word is *kerux,* a name ascribed to an imperial herald who made public the proclamation of an emperor's message, accompanied by due authority and the appropriate formality. The noun form of the word appears in II Timothy 4:2, which says, "Preach the word."

Those who are "appointed," or duly called of God, to preach the gospel should be glad to be known as "preachers." Paul was. Certainly there will be failures by some in the ministry, but we must keep in mind: there are no church failures, no gospel failures—only people failures! The truth stands tall, even when people fall low. People come and go, but the gospel lives on. The gospel message still works, the blood still flows from Calvary, and it still washes "whiter than snow"!

To be known as a preacher is better than to be known as a counselor, or an administrator, or a manager, or even a leader, although all those are noble titles. A person may be any or all of those and not be a preacher; but a preacher is all of those and more! A person may set his goal to excel in virtually any field and achieve it, but the preaching ministry is a definite calling that must not be chosen as though it were a vocation. Someone should not enter into it lightly, but by special invitation or definite direction from the Lord.

Pastors and evangelists should be marked by their preaching ministry (Acts 6:4; I Corinthians 1:18-24). Paul added that he was an apostle and "a teacher of the Gentiles." A preacher must also be "apt to teach" (I Timothy 3:2).

Verse 12. Paul experienced suffering as a result of his special calling (Philippians 1:29-30; II Corinthians 11:21-28), but he was never ashamed of his testimony or calling (Philippians 3:10; Romans 1:16). It gave him an opportunity to proclaim the power of God, which keeps those who commit everything—their lives, their liberty, their reputations, their eternity—into His hands.

Paul knew God personally. The word for "know" is *oida* (absolute knowledge, beyond doubt) instead of *ginosko* (experiential knowledge), and it underscores the certainty of his faith. Wuest made this observation:

> The knowledge here is not personal knowledge gained by experience, such as fellowship with God, but a knowledge of what God is in Himself which makes Him absolutely dependable in any circumstances. "I have believed" is in the perfect tense in the Greek text. It is in its full meaning, "I have believed with the present result that my faith is a firmly settled one." It is like hammering a nail through a board and clinching it on the other side. It is there to stay.[2]

"Persuaded" is also in the perfect tense, indicating that Paul's faith was fixed and immovable. There was no moving him off of this settled assurance. "Keep" is *phylasso,* generally used in military parlance to indicate the status of being "guarded."

What did Paul mean by what he had "committed" to God—his soul or his service? Scholars are divided on the issue. Certainly he had committed the eternal salvation of his soul to the Lord, but he may also have referred to the service he had performed, since "that day" would likely refer to the future judgment when his works would be tried by fire (I Corinthians 3:13-15). "Committed" is a banking term meaning "to deposit." His faith had been put on deposit for salvation, and his works of service on deposit against the judgment. Paul probably had both salvation and service in mind in verse 9 when he spoke of the "holy calling," so the same could be true here.

C. Faithfulness in Suffering (1:13-14)

(13) Hold fast the form of sound words, which thou hast heard of me, in faith and love which is in Christ Jesus. (14) That good thing which was committed unto thee keep by the Holy Ghost which dwelleth in us.

Verse 13. "Form" is *hupotuposis,* meaning a mark left by a blow, such as a horse's hoof in the sand or the impression of a seal. Such a "pattern" could be duplicated. That is precisely what Paul had in mind. Timothy was to walk as he had walked, teach what he had taught, serve as he had served. He was to be entirely faithful to the doctrinal truths handed to him by the apostle, having faith and love in Jesus Christ. "In faith and love" are modifiers of "hold fast." (See Ephesians 4:13-15.)

Verse 14. Paul had committed the deposit of truth to Timothy, and Timothy was to guard (*phylasso,* to guard, watch, defend) the deposit with the utmost care. Guarding the truth is an awesome responsibility. It is tragic when even the crumbs of truth that some denominations have held to tenaciously for so long are compromised and set aside. Many have despised and forsaken what once gave them their distinctiveness, for fear of "offending others who may not see it just like that." The body of Christ must continue to hand the torch of truth faithfully from generation to generation.

The noted explorers Lewis and Clark visited the Mandan Indian settlements in the Dakotas in the early 1800s. They discovered some interesting facts and legends about this tribe. They were possibly the descendants of "white Indians" who supposedly migrated from Wales about one thousand years before but over the course of time had virtually lost their heritage. The elders knew precious little of their religious roots, only that there had been a flood over all the earth and a great canoe had saved a few of the men and animals from drowning. They knew of a dove that had been sent to search for land. They knew of a Great Spirit whose son had come to live on the earth and been killed, only to come back to life. But no one could remember his name! They had been pushed farther into the interior of the continent by native Indians, "gradually becoming less Welsh and more Indian and forgetting how to read or speak their Celtic tongue, forgetting the name and nature of their Christian God. Imagine a people ever forgetting who they were. Imagine a people ever forgetting who their God was."[3] Within thirty years of Lewis and Clark's visit, practically all of the Mandans were wiped out by a disease (likely smallpox) that swept their villages. Today only a few artifacts and sketchy testimonies remain to mark their existence.

This saga underscores the importance of passing the faith along to one's children, friends, and kin. The early church was evangelical. The great Christian movements throughout the ages have been evangelical. The church today must be evangelical. That means not only loving and holding fast to the tenets of the faith but also passing them on. We need only lose one generation to break the chain—and who would remember the Lord or His name?

We must one day account for what has been faithfully delivered to us. Ezra selected twelve couriers to deliver 650 talents of silver and 100 talents of gold, along with gold and silver vessels, to the house of the Lord in Jerusalem. When they arrived each piece was carefully weighed to be sure everything that had been committed to them was still there (Ezra 8:24-34). We must also give an account of our stewardship (Luke 16:2; I Peter 4:5; Romans 14:12; Hebrews 13:17). To whom much is given, much shall be required (Luke 12:48).

D. As One Deserted (1:15)

(15) This thou knowest, that all they which are in Asia be turned away from me; of whom are Phygellus and Hermogenes.

Verse 15. How sad it must have made Paul to have to say, "Everyone in Asia has turned away from me." Regardless of the reason, it is very traumatic to be rejected. Paul evidently had some very lonely moments.

135

Most scholars believe that the apostle had reference to a mass departure from the faith and not a personal rejection of Paul himself. However, he did say "me." He took it partly personal. There always seems to be a tinge of guilt or self-doubt in the minds of preachers when believers backslide and depart the faith. "Did I do all that I could have done? Where did I fail?" Those are common questions that, doubtless, Paul entertained in his more reflective moments.

Perhaps Paul indulged in hyperbole (deliberate exaggeration as a figure of speech) when he said *all* had forsaken him. When did everyone forsake Paul? The full story is not known, and some speculate that he referred to his second arrest and ensuing confinement in Rome. In this context, the "turning away" would mean that most of his friends would not stand with him when he faced the rulers of Rome, and perhaps the emperor himself, to defend himself (4:16).

The naming of two specific individuals here, and the subsequent inclusion of two others in 2:17, lends strength to the interpretation that the "turning away" may have been related to doctrinal problems. Perhaps these four were leaders in the apostasy that infiltrated the churches of the region.

Paul did not refer to the vast continent of modern Asia, but to a Roman province in the western portion of Asia Minor, in what is Turkey today. Ephesus was its capital.

E. Aided by a Friend (1:16-18)

(16) The Lord give mercy unto the house of Onesiphorus; for he oft refreshed me, and was not ashamed of

*my chain: (17) but, when he was in Rome, he sought me
out very diligently, and found me. (18) The Lord grant unto
him that he may find mercy of the Lord in that day; and
in how many things he ministered unto me at Ephesus,
thou knowest very well.*

Verses 16-18. God has a tremendous compensation
plan! There always seems to be a balance available for
us in life. When there is an exodus from the truth, and
the majority seems to reject its advocate, God sends someone along to fill the gap and make up the hedge. In Paul's
experience, this gap filler was Onesiphorus. When others
forsook him, this kind man was at his side. His ministry
to Paul was timely—he "oft refreshed" him, perhaps open-
ing his home as a stopover for Paul on his journeys. When
Paul was in Rome, Onesiphorus sought him out—not only
sought, but found him—to render aid, presumably at great
personal risk.

Onesiphorus was not ashamed of Paul's status as a
prisoner. He evidently knew the enormous value of the
apostle to the church and desired to see his effectiveness
persevere indefinitely. He went out of his way to see that
the man of God did not lack.

God takes note of those who hold up the hands of the
preacher. He honored the efforts of Aaron and Hur to
support the arms of Moses by turning the tide of the battle in the favor of the Israelites (Exodus 17:10-13). People like Onesiphorus will receive rewards at the judgment
seat of Christ (I Corinthians 3). They may not be great
pulpit orators or turn cities to Christ, but they are servers,
givers, and helpers. Paul took time to recognize those who
assisted him in the gospel work. (Romans 16 is a classic

example.) He even included "helps" (I Corinthians 12:28) as one of the gifts of Christ to the church. Onesiphorus certainly fit well into that category of ministry, and Paul expressed confidence that God would reward him greatly.

Footnotes

[1]Vincent, 291.

[2]Wuest, *The Pastoral Epistles in the Greek New Testament* (Grand Rapids: Eerdmans, 1954), 123.

[3]James A. Thom, *From Sea to Shining Sea* (New York: Ballantine Books, 1984), 641.

II TIMOTHY
Chapter Two

IV. Occupations of the Christian (2:1-26)

A. A Steward (2:1-2)
(1) Thou therefore, my son, be strong in the grace that is in Christ Jesus. (2) And the things that thou hast heard of me among many witnesses, the same commit thou to faithful men, who shall be able to teach others also.

Verse 1. This chapter, uses eight cogent illustrations to depict the Christian life. The first is that of a son (*teknon,* child). It is an affectionate term, not limited to reference to children. To be strong in grace is to trust completely in the care and keeping power of Jesus. It is to depend totally upon Him to fulfill every promise, to realize that one's strength comes only from a higher spiritual source. Many Bible writers referred to the strength of the Lord as the supernatural source of sustenance—Moses (Exodus 13:3); David (Psalm 27:1); Jeremiah (16:19); Habakkuk (3:19); Paul (Ephesians 3:16; II Timothy 4:17); Peter (I Peter 5:10).

Verse 2. Paul returned to a frequent theme in the Pastorals, that of preserving and transmitting the traditions of truth. In view of the nearness of his death, he wanted to be sure that the gospel was preserved intact for future generations. He constantly reminded his co-workers to be faithful to the truth. Every Christian today owes much to his insistence on faithfulness.

Not only is truth to be held, loved, and preached, it is to be transmitted to "faithful men." Ministers should work especially with trustworthy individuals with potential, developing and discipling them fully, so that they may in turn teach the principles of the kingdom to others. It is difficult, if not impossible, to disciple large numbers of people or an entire congregation at once. It is advisable to focus on smaller groups where individual attention can be given, bring a small contingent to maturity, and then press upon them the necessity to assist in the maturation of others. Helping to disciple others will hasten one's own spiritual growth, creating a continuing cycle of blessing.

The apostle desired to establish an apostolic succession based on Christian teaching rather than one of administration. He was not concerned here with handing leadership in the church to a specific successor, but with preserving truth and ethical teaching.

B. A Soldier (2:3-4)

(3) Thou therefore endure hardness, as a good soldier of Jesus Christ. (4) No man that warreth entangleth himself with the affairs of this life; that he may please him who hath chosen him to be a soldier.

Verse 3. Here is another figure to illustrate the Christian life—that of a soldier. The life of a soldier, someone who is engaged in warfare in behalf of another, is never easy. He has hardships to endure. He is away from home and family for periods of time. His time is not his own. He must conform to certain standards and disciplines. He is required to carry a weighty burden of weapons and tools. His food is not always in sufficient quantity or quality. He is in constant danger. Sufferings and adversities are daily possibilities. These problems are easily applicable to the life of the Christian in general and the minister in particular.

One of the more positive perspectives of the view of the Christian as a soldier is that he is not alone. Usually he is part of a larger company engaged in the same battle. Thus the Greek term here, *sunkakopatheo,* means "to endure with someone else." Paul himself had endured hardship; therefore Timothy should expect to endure it also. Paul did not ask the younger preacher to do something he himself, or their Commander-in-Chief, would not do. "Be ye followers of me, even as I also am of Christ" (I Corinthians 11:1). We are never alone in our battle (Joshua 1:5; Matthew 28:20; II Corinthians 4:9; Hebrews 13:5).

Verse 4 carries the military metaphor a little further: the soldier cuts any entangling ties with civilian life. "Warreth" is *strateuo,* "to be on active duty in the military service." "Affairs" is *pragmateia,* "the discharging of business or occupational matters." A man cannot be a soldier and a civilian at the same time. He must leave the pursuits of one to discharge the duties of the other. Jesus alluded to this principle in Luke 17:33: "Whosoever shall seek to save his life shall lose it; and whosoever shall lose his life [for my sake] shall preserve it." We cannot serve two masters; we must choose a single path to walk.

141

If we say, "I want to do whatever I desire without moral or ethical restrictions," then we may, but we must be willing to pay the price for that decision. The person who says, "I willingly surrender my life—my time, my energies, my abilities, my resources—to the Lord Jesus," in effect "losing" his life, will receive the reward of abundant, eternal life (Matthew 19:29).

C. An Athlete (2:5)

(5) And if a man also strive for masteries, yet is he not crowned, except he strive lawfully.

Verse 5 compares the Christian life to engaging in athletics. To "strive" (*athleo,* to contest or contend in public games) means to compete for the prize (I Corinthians 9:24-25; Philippians 3:14). The prize is fruitful service in this life and, ultimately, eternal life.

But there is one major qualification: one must strive "lawfully" (*nominos,* to keep the rules of the game). Those who insist on breaking the rules are disqualified. The Greek athlete was required to participate in a rigorous training schedule of exercises, a special diet, and a review of the rules governing the event(s). Should he break training rules, he would be considered a "castaway" (*adokimos,* disqualified, barred from participating in the games) (I Corinthians 9:27). The victor's crown will never be placed on a rebel's head! He chooses his own way; he disregards the regulations or merely makes up his own as he goes. He will be disappointed at the judgment seat of Christ.

D. A Farmer (2:6-7)

(6) The husbandman that laboureth must be first partaker of the fruits. (7) Consider what I say; and the Lord give thee understanding in all things.

Verse 6. Now the passage turns to the metaphor of the farmer. A "husbandman" (*georgos*) is a farmer, literally a "tiller of the soil." Perhaps this is one of the best examples of the work of the preacher. Jesus used it in Matthew 13:3. The preacher sows the word in the hearts of the hearers, trusts that the seed falls on good ground, waits for the harvest, and rejoices when it comes. He then is entitled to the first fruits of his labors, taking the first share of the crop for himself and his family.

God expects the spiritual farmer, the pastor, to be rewarded for his hard work. He who preaches the gospel faithfully need not be reticent about accepting his just dues. He who preaches the gospel may live of the gospel, deriving his financial support from the Lord's service. (See I Corinthians 9:1-19.) Speaking of financial remuneration, the Bible says that the teaching elders are worthy of double honor. (See the commentary on I Timothy 5:17-18.)

Verse 7. In using metaphors and allegories, Paul trusted that Timothy understood what he was saying. He wanted Timothy to meditate on his words, and if he did, God would give him full understanding. God told Joshua to meditate in the law night and day (Joshua 1:8). David said the delight of the "blessed man" is "the law of the LORD; and in his law doth he meditate day and night" (Psalm 1:2).

One does not find four-leaf clovers by running through the fields; he must get down on his hands and knees, gently parting the blades and leaves of grass. By the same token, one does not discover deep truths by racing through life or hurrying through the Bible. Understanding and wisdom come only to the person who diligently searches for them—"If you accept my words and store up my commands within you, turning your ear to wisdom and applying your heart to understanding, and if you call out for insight and cry aloud for understanding, and if you look for it as for silver and search for it as for hidden treasure, then you will understand the fear of the LORD and find the knowledge of God. For the LORD gives wisdom, and from his mouth come knowledge and understanding" (Proverbs 2:1-6, NIV). If we meditate on the word of God, we will find in it understanding and the knowledge of God.

E. An Instructor (2:8-14)

(8) Remember that Jesus Christ of the seed of David was raised from the dead according to my gospel: (9) wherein I suffer trouble, as an evil doer, even unto bonds; but the word of God is not bound. (10) Therefore I endure all things for the elect's sakes, that they may also obtain the salvation which is in Christ Jesus with eternal glory. (11) It is a faithful saying: For if we be dead with him, we shall also live with him: (12) if we suffer, we shall also reign with him; if we deny him, he also will deny us: (13) if we believe not, yet he abideth faithful: he cannot deny himself. (14) Of these things put them in remembrance, charging them before the Lord that they strive not about words to no profit, but to the subverting of the hearers.

Verse 8. Jesus Christ is our example in all of these areas. He Himself was faithful as a son, a soldier, an athlete, and a farmer. He did not turn away from hardship or the specter of death. He willingly gave His life (Philippians 2:5-9; I Peter 2:23). He strove lawfully; therefore He is crowned with glory and honor (Hebrews 2:9).

The "seed of David" speaks of His humanity; "raised from the dead" indicates His deity. It is not a dead Christ we are to meditate on, but a living, resurrected Lord! Some groups within Christendom consistently portray Christ as dead or dying, on a cross or being taken down from it. Others seem to worship a God who resides in a distant, ethereal corner of heaven, untouchable, unapproachable—"out there somewhere, but not in touch with our present lives." But we can know the Lord as Paul did: "Christ in you, the hope of glory" (Colossians 1:27).

The use of the Greek perfect participle for "raised" indicates that the completed action of the past is still in effect presently—He is raised and still alive! That is the "good news" of the gospel Paul preached.

Verse 9. The preaching of the resurrection brought persecution to Paul and other bold Christians of his day. He submitted to a considerable list of indignities heaped upon him for his witness of Christ (II Corinthians 11:24-28). Jesus never said Christians would be exempt from trouble. People hated Him; they shall hate us (Luke 6:22; John 15:18; I John 3:13). They persecuted Him; they will persecute us (Matthew 5:44; John 15:20; I Corinthians 4:12). But He will keep us through the trouble (II Corinthians 4:7-11)! We will suffer while in enemy territory and should expect it and endure it as a good soldier!

"Evil doer" is *kakourgos,* "criminal." That Paul

persecuted Christians did not make him a criminal in the eyes of the Jews, but preaching the gospel did! As a Christian, Paul was not an evildoer, but he suffered as though he had been the lowest sort of felon or murderer. Nevertheless, while he was bound, the Word of God was not shackled! Paul preached with chains on his hands to rulers (Acts 26:27-29), he witnessed on board doomed ships (Acts 27:21-26), and he shared the gospel even in prison itself (Acts 16:27-33). Because of his persecution the gospel went to many places it would never have gone otherwise. That is why he could testify that "the things which have happened unto me have fallen out rather unto the furtherance of the gospel; so that my bonds in Christ are manifest in all the palace, and in all other places" (Philippians 1:12-13).

Verse 10. Paul was willing to "endure all things" to get the gospel to all the world. He was a driven man. No price was too great to pay: "None of these things move me, neither count I my life dear unto myself" (Acts 20:24). His whole self was dedicated to one cause—preaching the gospel to the lost and building up the household of faith (the elect). His suffering was not vicarious as was Christ's suffering and did not provide salvation for people, but it occurred in the process of reaching them with the truth— "that they may also obtain salvation which is in Christ Jesus with eternal glory." When they witnessed the price he paid to bring them the gospel it encouraged them and incited them to deeper commitment and service. He would endure anything to see people saved.

Verse 11. This verse introduces a promise related to the preceding statement of the eternal glories of those who are saved. The use of "for" shows the connection.

If we have died with Christ, we shall also live with Him.

"It is a faithful saying," or a "trustworthy word" (*logos*, thought or concept), a fact we can count on. If we have freely surrendered our lives totally to Him ("dead with him"), it follows that we shall also live with Him! Romans 6 explains this concept further. "I die daily" was Paul's testimony to the Corinthians (I Corinthians 15:31). He was a walking dead man! He implored the Romans to offer themselves likewise: "I beseech you therefore, brethren, by the mercies of God, that ye present your bodies a living sacrifice, holy, acceptable unto God, which is your reasonable service" (Romans 12:1). The Christian who reckons himself dead to the world, self, and sin will live unto Christ in this life and possess the hope of eternal life.

Verse 12. The subject of the context is still suffering (verses 3, 9). If there is suffering to endure, so be it, for we will reign with Christ later. Our suffering for truth will witness for us in the judgment.

We suffer in different ways. Some are rejected by their friends and families when they come to Christ (Matthew 10:35-37). Others lose their social status (Philippians 3:7-8). Still others are called on to suffer physically (Acts 7:54-60; II Corinthians 11:23-28). Suffering for righteousness' sake and keeping the faith through struggles is admirable. It adds an enhancing dimension to a person's life. He becomes more empathetic, more understanding, and more able to help those who are going through trials. A burl on a tree originates because of suffering—perhaps a limb broken off in a storm or some other trauma—and it usually has some of the most beautiful grain in the entire tree. It is coveted for knife handles and many small specialty items made from wood. We do not need to invite suffering, but we should not disdain it if it comes. It may be the making of a man of God!

"Deny" (*arneomai*) may be understood as "disown." If we do not acknowledge Christ as our own, He will not acknowledge us as His own. Peter was guilty of denying that he knew Christ, fearing that to claim Him would be tantamount to death. Later he was convicted in his heart and wept bitterly in contrite repentance. Others had a different spirit (I John 2:19; II Timothy 4:10) and will be judged accordingly. (See also Matthew 10:33; Luke 9:26.)

Verse 13. "Believe not" is from *apisteuo* and conveys the idea of unfaithfulness in addition to actual unbelief. Regardless of whether we are faithful in our Christian lives, Christ is going to remain faithful. He must remain true to His own nature and character. His faithfulness is eternal. (See Isaiah 49:13-16; Lamentations 3:23.)

Verse 14. "These things" probably refers to the content of verses 8-13. The minister is to proclaim these truths, and believers are to remember them. They are weighty matters, and meditation time should be given to them. By contrast, it is a waste of time to split theological hairs over matters that have no consequence. *Logomacheo* is literally "to contend about words" and can be paraphrased as "wrangling about trifling matters." The result of such argument is that people become confused and dismayed. They are likely to lose faith or be deceived by the perfidy of semantics. (See the commentary on Titus 3:9.)

F. A Student (2:15-19)

(15) Study to show thyself approved unto God, a workman that needeth not to be ashamed, rightly dividing

*the word of truth. (16) But shun profane and vain bab-
blings: for they will increase unto more ungodliness.
(17) And their word will eat as doth a canker: of whom
is Hymenaeus and Philetus; (18) who concerning the truth
have erred, saying that the resurrection is past already;
and overthrow the faith of some. (19) Nevertheless the foundation of God standeth sure, having this seal, The Lord
knoweth them that are his. And, Let every one that nameth
the name of Christ depart from iniquity.*

Verse 15. "Study" is from *spoudazo,* meaning "give
diligence to." The word does not have exclusive reference
to studying as in reading books, but describes a workman's exertion to do a job well. It does not totally exclude
the study of books in that it certainly takes diligent study
to become an unashamed workman who is skilled in
"rightly dividing" the word of truth.

Every Christian, and especially every minister, ought
to be a lifelong student. One never reaches a plateau in
the process of learning. There are three foundations of
learning: seeing much, suffering much, and studying
much. The person who would escape ignorance keeps his
eyes and ears open. He is observant. Thus he discovers
the reasons for and consequences of people's actions. To
suffer much is to experience the ebb and flow of life, to
encounter its highs and lows, to know by doing, touching,
tasting. Studying much can be "a weariness of the flesh"
(Eccesiastes 12:12) but also a delight to one who hungers
for knowledge and truth. Even in Paul's last days he asked
Timothy to bring his books and parchments (II Timothy
4:13), having reminded him earlier to "give attendance
to reading" (I Timothy 4:13). No one is educated in the

fullest sense who is not a reader. Seeing, suffering, studying—together they make a whole person. Such a person not only knows how, but he also knows why—and while a person who only knows how will always have a job, the man who also knows why will always be his boss!

To "rightly divide" (*orthotomeo,* to cut a straight course) the Word of God means to interpret it correctly, or "lay out a road which cuts straight through," not giving way to detours of skepticism or higher criticism. The Greek word was often used of a stonemason when he cut stones straight and square to fit neatly into the building. The NEB translates it as "cutting a straight furrow." Since Paul was a tentmaker, he knew the importance of "cutting it straight." That the whole Bible is true, without contradictions, can be clearly seen when it is cut straight, interpreted correctly, and rightly laid out.

A good example is to observe that the four Gospels present the coming of Christ (His birth, life, teachings, death, burial, resurrection, and ascension); the Book of Acts reveals how the church was founded and how people were born again to enter the church; the Epistles are written to saved believers, guiding them in Christian doctrine and lifestyle; and the Book of Revelation gives us a glimpse into the future of the church and the world. Understanding the New Testament in that perspective enables us to interpret clearly some of the more difficult passages.

"Cutting it straight" also encompasses handling the Word sincerely, without hypocrisy, deceit, or trickery (II Corinthians 4:2; I Thessalonians 2:2-6). It means not adding or taking away anything (Revelation 22:18-19), treating the Word fairly, without abridgment, believing it in its entirety, and accepting it all as the revealed will of God.

Verse 16. By contrast—"but" (*de*)—we are to avoid profane and empty talk. Unbelief loves to express itself. Doubt enjoys maximum exposure. We are to shun them; otherwise, more doubt and unbelief—"ungodliness"—is the result. (See the commentary on I Timothy 6:20.)

Verse 17. Another reason for avoiding such words is that they insidiously eat like a canker (a cancerous growth) or pollute like gangrene. The Greek word is *gaggraina*, "cancer, gangrene." The more false teachers are tolerated the more they will poison the well. They will corrupt the body of Christ. Evidently Hymenaeus and Philetus were conspicuously of that number. While professing to be part of the church they were in fact destroying it. Their teachings were sources of spiritual disease and death. Hymenaeus was probably the man excommunicated in I Timothy 1:20.

Verse 18. The particular doctrine in which they had "erred" was the resurrection of the dead. They said it had occurred already. Probably they spiritualized the resurrection as being salvation itself. Timothy was to avoid disputing with these men and others like them, realizing they had "erred" (*astocheo*, to miss the mark) and could be turned neither by reason, patience, nor love. It is vain to enter into semantical battles with such people. They can easily overthrow the faith of Christians who may not be well grounded in the truth. Erdmen commented:

The serious influence of these errors may not
be realized until one reads the fifteenth chapter

of First Corinthians, in which Paul shows that a belief in a future resurrection of believers is inseparable from a belief in the resurrection of Christ, which he declares to be the very foundation stone of the Christian faith; and in this chapter he shows further the perilous results of abandoning these beliefs. Thus Paul here declares that the effect of "saying that the resurrection is past already," is to "overthrow the faith of some."[1]

It is dangerous to give ministers wide latitude with respect to serious doctrinal errors. Error, like a canker, leads to more error. It spreads until the whole body is affected and is in jeopardy of missing the mark. The church that says, "Come with us, brother, and don't worry about whether your convictions and doctrines are in line with ours; our only creed is Christ, and we don't split hairs over doctrinal matters" is in grave danger of becoming something other than a church. God's church cares about doctrinal purity. The Pastorals prove that over and over again.

Verse 19. People may fail, err doctrinally, or stumble morally. That is why we must build on the foundation of Christ (I Corinthians 3:11). If we do that, we will not become involved in apostasy or heresy. If we build on people, trust them to have all the answers, and put confidence in the flesh, we will find that our foundation is sand. Some depart from the faith because they were not built on the right foundation (I John 2:19). They trusted in themselves and their own human wisdom. Such departure does not weaken the foundation of God, however. It is not shifting, cracked, or in danger of collapse.

People come and go, philosophies come and go, theories come and go, but the foundation of truth remains steady and faithful. Jesus is the truth (John 14:6), and He remains faithful (II Timothy 2:13). That is why complete and unfeigned trust in Jesus Christ is the way of salvation.

Some view the foundation spoken of here as the church. It is true that we "are built upon the foundation of the apostles and prophets, Jesus Christ himself being the chief corner stone" (Ephesians 2:20). The church is founded by God (Matthew 16:18), and it stands firm despite the waywardness and defections of some of its members. Nevertheless, it seems that in the context, this verse refers primarily to Jesus Himself as the foundation.

The foundation has this "seal," literally, it "is sealed with this [twofold] inscription": "The Lord knoweth them that are his" and "Let every one that nameth the name of Christ depart from iniquity." Vincent elaborated: "There are two inscriptions on the foundation stone, the one guaranteeing the *security,* the other the *purity,* of the church. The two go together. The purity of the church is indispensable to its security."[2]

Concerning His sheep, Jesus said, "I know them . . . and they shall never perish" (John 10:27-28). What a consolation! With this promise we encourage ourselves and others to remain faithful and to "depart from iniquity." Being known of the Lord does not give us license to take advantage of our liberty but should motivate us to purity.

G. A Vessel (2:20-22)

(20) But in a great house there are not only vessels of gold and of silver, but also of wood and of earth; and some to honour, and some to dishonour. (21) If a man therefore

purge himself from these, he shall be a vessel unto honour, sanctified, and meet for the master's use, and prepared unto every good work. (22) Flee also youthful lusts: but follow righteousness, faith, charity, peace, with them that call on the Lord out of a pure heart.

Verse 20. The chapter turns to another figure—that of a vessel in a large house. There are certain vessels (dishes, pots) made of expensive material (gold, silver), which are used only on special occasions. There are also vessels made of inexpensive materials (wood, clay), which are designed for mundane or even unclean activities.

Verse 21. We come in contact with people who fit both descriptions. The message is that we are to strive to be a vessel of honor. We can do that by "purging" ourselves from the vessels of dishonor, by avoiding close association with persons whose only benefit is to serve as a warning and and an example of the possibilities of apostasy. The person who keeps himself from contamination by false teachers and spiritual error makes himself "meet" (fit) for the master's use. "Prepared" is *hetoimazo*, prepared in the sense of being "equipped."

Avoiding defilement by heretical elements in the professing church should be a goal of every young minister and of every saint of God. Fellowship with the unfruitful works of darkness will defile. Rather than having fellowship with them we should reprove them (Ephesians 5:11). That does not mean we should have no evangelistic contact with them, but there is a vast difference between evangelism and fellowship.

Verse 22. Having warned Timothy of the sins of apostasy, Paul now cautioned against falling prey to the sins of the flesh. The Christian is to remain morally pure in the midst of a perverse and licentious generation. Opportunities to transgress may abound, but the wise person will actively avoid fornication, adultery, and other sins of the body and spirit (Galatians 5:19-21).

Youthful lusts (*epithumia,* a craving, a passionate desire) may not be restricted to sexual attractions. Youth tend toward unrealistic idealism. They are plagued by impractical objectives. Their wants and wishes often far outstrip their needs. The useless pursuit of fame, or money, or things presses them. In essence, this verse reminds us that the most important things in life are not things.

We are to "follow" (*dioko,* pursue, seek to manifest, stronger than the English "follow") the Christian graces of righteousness, faith, love, and peace. Such pursuit should be done in the company of those who share the same objectives. We are to have fellowship with the vessels of honor and purge ourselves from the vessels of dishonor.

H. A Servant (2:23-26)

(23) But foolish and unlearned questions avoid, knowing that they do gender strifes. (24) And the servant of the Lord must not strive; but be gentle unto all men, apt to teach, patient, (25) in meekness instructing those that oppose themselves; if God peradventure will give them repentance to the acknowledging of the truth; (26) and that they may recover themselves out of the snare of the devil, who are taken captive by him at his will.

Verse 23. Again the epistle admonishes us to avoid foolish questions and discussions that serve no good purpose. (See verse 16.) Too often these discussions lead to disagreements and misunderstandings. The Greek word here is *machomai,* meaning "to argue with heated emotions, debate." Such interchanges generate more heat than light!

Verse 24. The minister should avoid such fights so as to remain gentle, manifesting an attitude of calm self-control and being patient. Arguing is not teaching, and being "apt to teach" is a basic qualification for the minister. Obsession or preoccupation with foolish or novel questions diminishes that aptitude.

Verse 25. The minister is to gently instruct (persuade, guide, correct) those who oppose him. (They actually oppose themselves because they lead themselves away from the saving truth.) It is possible that through such gentle instruction God will give them a change of mind—"repentance" (a change of mind from false ideas to acknowledging the truth). Godly sorrow leads to repentance (II Corinthians 7:9-10), but repentance is more than contrition. It involves submission of one's will and mind to the truth.

Verse 26. The emphasis here is that those who have turned from the truth may return to the graces of God ("to their senses," NASB; "to soberness," Alford). False teaching is the snare of the devil. He was the first to use it (in the Garden of Eden), and he has duped people with error and lies throughout the centuries so that they may share in his own condemnation (I Timothy 3:6). False doctrines hold people captive. Sound teaching sets them free.

Footnotes

[1]Erdman, 118.
[2]Vincent, 304.

II TIMOTHY
Chapter Three

V. Enduring in the End Time (3:1-17)

A. Perilous Times (3:1)
(1) This know also, that in the last days perilous times shall come.

Verse 1. "The last days" probably include the entire church age, extending from Pentecost until the present time. Although these conditions may escalate and proliferate in the end time, they did exist in Timothy's day, for Paul instructed him, "From such turn away" (verse 5).

"Perilous" is *chalepos,* literally "hard" times, when it will be difficult to maintain one's own spiritual equilibrium as well as be successful in persuading others to submit themselves to God. Particular pressures will be evident in the end time. Spiritual drowsiness is always a possibility in the midnight hour. Subtle dangers will present themselves to Christians just before the coming of the Lord. We must be aware, alert, and knowledgeable of the wiles of the devil.

B. The Temptations of Flesh and Spirit (3:2-5)

(2) For men shall be lovers of their own selves, covetous, boasters, proud, blasphemers, disobedient to parents, unthankful, unholy, (3) without natural affection, trucebreakers, false accusers, incontinent, fierce, despisers of those that are good, (4) traitors, heady, highminded, lovers of pleasures more than lovers of God; (5) having a form of godliness, but denying the power thereof: from such turn away.

Verse 2. "Men" is from the generic word *anthropos,* meaning "mankind," encompassing the whole race, both male and female. Verses 2-4 list eighteen characteristics of people in the end time.

"Lovers of their own selves"—*philautos,* "lover of self." The rise of the cult of self-love in our day has been phenomenal. It is the heart of the New Age beliefs, as well as the New Thought proponents, Unitarian-Universalists, and many Eastern religious sects. We hear much of self-confidence, self-fulfillment, self-actualization, self-motivation, and many other compound ideas beginning with self. Self is on the throne in many hearts—"I am the Master of my fate, I am the Captain of my soul" (*Invictus,* Tennyson). People become introspective in search of truth, thinking that they can discover divinity there. The idea that "men are gods but just haven't recognized it yet" pervades our world. Pantheism is again flowering in the present age. It is a sign of the end!

"Covetous"—*philarguros,* from *phileo* (to love) and *arguros*(silver), thus "lover of money." Money, or the means of exchange, is not sinful in itself, but loving it is still the "root of all evil" (I Timothy 6:10). Loving it will pervert our thinking. Our power of reason will fail us. Temptation will overcome us. Jesus said, "Ye cannot serve God and mammon" (Matthew 6:24). For this reason, the Bible stresses the importance of contentment (Philippians 4:11; I Timothy 6:8; Hebrews 13:5). God hated covetousness from the beginning and included its condemnation in the Ten Commandments (Exodus. 20:17).

"Boasters"—*alazones,* "imposters, braggarts, pretenders." Such persons often profess the faith but do not have fruit to back up their profession. (See I Corinthians 13:4; James 4:16.)

"Proud"—*huperephanos,* "to show above." Many translations render this word as "haughty." Such a person thinks more of himself than is merited, particularly thinking he is above others. As Ernest Legouve once said, "If he could only see how small a vacancy his death would leave, the proud man would think less of the place he occupies in his lifetime." God puts this sin at the top of the list of the things he hates (Proverbs 6:17; 8:13). It is the threshold to many other transgressions. The inimitable John Ruskin observed:

I have been more and more convinced, the more I think of it, that, in general, pride is at the bottom of all great mistakes. All the other passions do occasional good; but whenever pride puts in its word, everything goes wrong; and what it might really be desirable to do, quietly and innocently, it is mortally dangerous to do proudly.

(See also Proverbs 16:18; James 4:6; I Peter 5:5; I John 2:16.)

"Blasphemers"—*blasphemos,* "evil speaker, slanderer, reviler." Blasphemy in the sense of a believer persistently reviling, slandering, and rejecting the Holy Spirit is unpardonable (Matthew 12:31-32) because he cuts himself off from the only means God has to deal with him, but blasphemy committed by an unbeliever in ignorance can be forgiven (I Timothy 1:13).

"Disobedient to parents"—rejecting parental authority. This sin defines a large segment of the present generation. Honoring one's mother and father is the first commandment with promise (Deuteronomy 5:16; Ephesians 6:2) and was enjoined by Paul (Ephesians 6:1; Colossians 3:20). Solomon admonished his readers to "keep thy father's commandment, and forsake not the law of thy mother" (Proverbs 6:20). (See also Leviticus 19:3; Deuteronomy 27:16; Proverbs 23:22; Luke 18:20.) Under Old Testament law a rebellious son was to be stoned to death (Deuteronomy 21:18-21). Were that statute enforced today, virtually a whole generation would disappear from the earth!

"Unthankful"—*acharistos,* "ungrateful." Who can enjoy the highest living standard the world has ever known without being thankful? Who can sit down and eat his meal and never give a thought to the ultimate Provider? Only selfish brutes who have no sense of appreciation for life or breath! A hog can eat acorns under an oak tree but cannot look up to see where they came from. His ears cover his eyes. He has to be placed on his back in order to look up!

"Unholy"—*anosios,* "irreligious, impious," a person who has no fellowship with God or relation to what is holy. It is an accurate depiction of today's secular humanist.

Verse 3. "Without natural affection"—*astorgos,* "without normal human love." Such a person does not care for those of his own household, but he may direct base affections to a friend, quite often someone of the same sex. Perversion in one area of life can lead to perversion in other areas. The same word appears in Romans 1:31 in a discussion on sexual perversion and reprobation.

"Trucebreakers"—*aspondos,* "irreconcilable, implacable, merciless." These people refuse to enter into a treaty or agreement and, if they did, would be suspect concerning its neglect.

"False accusers"—*diabolos,* the word usually used for the devil, "a slanderer" (Revelation 12:10). This kind of person will lie about a colleague in order to get his job, or slander another church member to make himself look a little better in the eyes of the pastor, or tell a falsehood about a competitor in order to win a contract. (See I Timothy 3:11.)

"Incontinent"—*akrates,* "without power over oneself," particularly relating to sensual lusts. It means "without strength," indicating a person who is easily led into degrading sins. Such a person is easily persuaded or deceived into committing evil. Needless murders and violent sex crimes are perpetrated by incontinent persons.

"Fierce"—*anemeros,* "untamed, savage." It is possible that a person could be both incontinent and fierce at the same time—incontinently indulging himself and being inhumane to others.

"Despisers of those which are good"—*aphilagathos,* "haters of good." Such people are more likely to appreciate a public criminal, a sexual offender, or a thrice-married woman than a wholesome, honest, hardworking person—especially if the shady character is a celebrity. Our society tends to make heroes out of the least deserving persons.

Verse 4. "Traitors"—*prodotes,* "a betrayer," one who may make a promise or a covenant but will go back on his word if it seems to serve his own interests. The word is used of Judas Iscariot in Luke 6:16.

"Heady"—*propetes,* "falling forward, headlong." It came to mean "hasty, rash," and it can describe someone who is reckless, bent on following a precipitous path to destruction.

"Highminded"—*tuphoomai,* "swollen with pride," from *tuphoo,* "to raise a smoke, wrap in a mist." A more modern term is "to put on airs." This person is conceited.

"Lovers of pleasures more than lovers of God"—*philedonos,* "given over to pleasure," specifies those persons who follow the philosophy of "eat, drink, and be merry, for tomorrow we die." They say, in effect, "So what if God is not pleased with our lifestyle? We would rather please ourselves than God!" The early Romans' cry was, "Give us bread and the circus!" First on their list was to eat to their fill, then be entertained. Such a gluttonous, self-serving attitude marked their civilization for extinction. More modern terms for their philosophy are hedonism and existentialism.

Verse 5. Another last-day sign is having a form, but not the power, of godliness. Outward semblance is not the same as inward reality. A person may appear to be religious, but if his faith does not motivate him to be spiritually victorious, of what value is it? Sin and unbelief inside create an impotent emptiness. Churches may dot the landscape, but if they deny the power of God to save miraculously and deliver supernaturally, they are sounding brass and a tinkling symbol, whited sepulchres full of dead men's bones. By contrast, God's church is built of living stones (I Peter 2:5).

We are to avoid such persons or churches. We are not to have fellowship with them or aid them in their endeavors. We can use our time more efficiently by focusing on unevangelized sinners or developing committed Christians than by continuing to have fellowship with carnal apostates.

C. False Religion (3:6-9)

(6) For of this sort are they which creep into houses, and lead captive silly women laden with sins, led away with divers lusts, (7) ever learning, and never able to come to the knowledge of the truth. (8) Now as Jannes and Jambres withstood Moses, so do these also resist the truth: men of corrupt minds, reprobate concerning the faith. (9) But they shall proceed no further: for their folly shall be manifest unto all men, as theirs also was.

Verse 6. "Of this sort" indicates that from among the persons just named are those who "creep" (*enduno,* enter on the sly, worm in) to ply their deception. The idea is that by trickery and false pretenses they find a way to get into homes and exercise influence. Such subterfuge results in captivating and subjugating the minds of certain susceptible women (*gunaikarion,* a little woman, used derogatorily). Wuest commented, "One of the great virtues of womanhood, namely, that of trusting another, is turned into a weakness by Satan here. Eve was deceived. Adam sinned with his eyes wide open."[1]

Many cults and sects prey on women, especially single women. Christian women must be discerning in such matters so that they are not taken advantage of.

The "sins and lusts" are not necessarily of the sexual variety; "divers" indicates that the lusts are variegated. The implication is that their worldly wants and desires are easily exploited. Jamieson, Fausset, and Brown suggest: "Not only animal lusts, but passion for change in doctrine and manner of teaching; the running after fashionable men and fashionable tenets."[2]

Verse 7. Such women are "ever learning" new doctrines, ideas, and theories, but the false teachers never lead them to the knowledge of the truth. "This refers to the women led astray. One of the strange phenomena of our day is the great number of women going to all kinds of Bible studies and religious meetings, who seem to gravitate to strange doctrines and unorthodox ideas. They never come for the truth, that faith once delivered unto the saints, the old-fashioned fundamentals of the Bible."[3]

Verse 8. The prototypes of modern deceivers existed in ancient times. Jannes and Jambres are apparently the Egyptian magicians who opposed Moses in Exodus 7:11-22. According to Numenius, they were sacred scribes, a lower order of priests in Egypt who were skilled in magic. Some interpret the name Jannes from the Ethiopian language as "trickster" and Jambres as "juggler." (See also Acts 13:8.)

As these magicians resisted Moses in copying his miracles, the false teachers of the end time may also use "lying wonders" (II Thessalonians 2:9; Matthew 24:24) to deceive the spiritually weak. People whose minds are corrupted will resist the truth, despising the true faith because of its demands on their character. They are actually reprobate (*adokimos*, rejected, disapproved, disqualified) concerning the faith.

Verse 9. Such people will eventually come to an end of their effectiveness, because their insane folly ("dementia," *Expositor's*) will become increasingly evident. The church should pray for discernment, wisdom, and understanding to defeat the purveyors of doctrinal error.

D. Persecution for the Faith (3:10-13)

(10) But thou hast fully known my doctrine, manner of life, purpose, faith, longsuffering, charity, patience, (11) persecutions, afflictions, which came unto me at Antioch, at Iconium, at Lystra; what persecutions I endured: but out of them all the Lord delivered me. (12) Yea, and all that will live godly in Christ Jesus shall suffer persecution. (13) But evil men and seducers shall wax worse and worse, deceiving, and being deceived.

Verse 10. "Fully known" is *parakoloutheo*, translated in Luke 1:3 as "perfect understanding." Paul compared the formerly mentioned individuals with himself, not to boast, but to offer a contrast to one who knew his life well. The apostle invited scrutiny of any area of his life. Faithfulness includes soundness in doctrine, a blameless lifestyle, a set resolution to fulfill his role in ministry, unwavering faith, patience, selfless love, and endurance.

Verse 11. Such an armory of spiritual weapons virtually guarantees consistent personal victory, even in the face of "persecutions and afflictions." Paul enumerated three of the places where he endured especially severe persecutions—Antioch in Pisidia (Acts 13:14, 50-51);

Iconium (Acts 14:1-5); Lystra (Acts 14:6, 19). Timothy was well aware of them, since he was from Lystra, and Jews from Antioch and Iconium had stirred up the persecution there.

When Paul said that God "delivered me," he did not mean that God prevented suffering. To the contrary, he felt the full impact of the persecution. In Lystra, the people stoned him and left him for dead (Acts 14:19). Paul could take his place with the "others" in Hebrews 11:36 who were not delivered from persecution but were kept through it. God has two ways of dealing with storms: He can calm the storm, or He can keep us through the storm. Jesus comforted His disciples with these words: "In the world ye shall have tribulation: but be of good cheer; I have overcome the world" (John 16:33). He reassured Paul with this promise: "My grace is sufficient for thee" (II Corinthians 12:9).

Verse 12. All Christians must resolve to endure suffering for the name of the Lord. God does not allow it into our lives to cause us to fall but to strengthen us. It is the destiny of "all that will live godly." Not all will suffer as Paul did. Most today will never feel the lash of the cat-o'-nine-tails, or the impact of stones, or even be dragged into court to face charges connected with being a Christian. (One introspective believer once asked himself, "If I were tried for being a Christian, would there be enough evidence to convict me?") But all will suffer in some way. Some will experience rejection from their peers or ostracism by their families (Matthew 10:36; 19:29). Others will encounter pressure or harassment from their colleagues. Such suffering comes because of living "godly in Christ Jesus." (See also I Thessalonians 2:14; Philippians 3:8.)

I Corinthians 4:12-13 presents the Christian's response to persecution: "Being reviled, we bless; being persecuted, we suffer it; being defamed, we intreat." Jesus instructed His disciples in the Sermon on the Mount: "Ye have heard that it hath been said, An eye for an eye, and a tooth for a tooth: but I say unto you, That ye resist not evil: but whosoever shall smite thee on thy right cheek, turn to him the other also. And if any man will sue thee at the law, and take away thy coat, let him have thy cloke also. And whosoever shall compel thee to go a mile, go with him twain. . . . Love your enemies, bless them that curse you, do good to them that hate you, and pray for them which despitefully use you, and persecute you; that ye may be the children of your Father which is in heaven. . . . For if ye love them which love you, what reward have ye?" (Matthew 5:38-46). Jesus lived out those instructions Himself: "Who, when he was reviled, reviled not again; when he suffered, he threatened not; but committed himself to him that judgeth righteously" (I Peter 2:23).

Some "suffering" is not the result of holy living, however, but our ignorance or wrongdoing, which would qualify as a "fault" described in I Peter 2:19-20: "For this is thankworthy, if a man for conscience toward God endure grief, suffering wrongfully. For what glory is it, if, when ye be buffeted for your faults, ye shall take it patiently? but if, when ye do well, and suffer for it, ye take it patiently, this is acceptable with God." We must be careful not to invite the wrath of unbelievers upon our heads by a lack of wisdom, a self-righteous attitude, or some other wrong. "But let none of you suffer as a murderer, or as a thief, or as an evildoer, or as a busybody in other men's matters" (I Peter 4:15). "But and if ye suffer for righteousness' sake, happy are ye: and be not afraid of their terror, neither be troubled . . . having a good conscience; that, whereas they speak evil of you, as of evildoers, they may be ashamed that falsely accuse your good conversation in Christ. For it is better, if the will of God be so, that ye suffer for well doing, than for evil doing" (I Peter 3:14-17). Unjustified suffering is the only kind that brings glory to God (I Peter 4:12-16).

Verse 13. The situation will not improve. Evil people will grow worse and will continue to deceive one another and be deceived. Jamieson, Fausset, and Brown made the following observation about such people: "He who has once begun to deceive others, is the less easily able to recover himself from error, and the more easily embraces in turn the errors of others."[4]

"Seducers" comes from *goes,* "a charlatan, an imposter," often translated "conjurer." The magical arts were in prominence in Ephesus (Acts 19:19) and were often used to keep the masses in sway through fear, in much the same way that voodoo is used in many parts of the world today. Acts 8:9-11 and Acts 13:6-10 describe sorcerers who practiced those arts. Sorcery and "lying wonders" will accompany events in the end time (II Thessalonians 2:9-10; Revelation 13:15; 18:23; 22:15). The Christian must beware lest he himself is deceived by such wonders. For this reason the gift of "discerning of spirits" (I Corinthians 12:10) is vital to the church today. Paul made use of it on various occasions (Acts 13:6-11; 16:16-18).

E. The Means to Overcome (3:14-17)

(14) But continue thou in the things which thou hast learned and hast been assured of, knowing of whom thou hast learned them; (15) and that from a child thou hast known the holy scriptures, which are able to make thee wise unto salvation through faith which is in Christ Jesus. (16) All scripture is given by inspiration of God, and is profitable for doctrine, for reproof, for correction, for instruction in righteousness: (17) that the man of God may be perfect, throughly furnished unto all good works.

Verse 14. Some other ministers "swerved," "made shipwreck," and "erred" (I Timothy 1:6, 19; 6:21), but Paul encouraged Timothy to "continue" in the things that Paul himself, along with Lois and Eunice, had taught him. "Assured of" probably incorporates both the Scriptures (verses 15-16) and experience (II Timothy 1:6-7). Armed with truth and personal experience, one can stop the mouths of deceivers (Titus 1:11). It is often said that "a man with an argument is no match for a man with an experience." How much more effective as a Christian is a someone who has both the truth and an experience!

Verse 15. Timothy had been taught the Old Testament Scriptures as a young boy. As he used them as a guide to put the teachings of Christianity into perspective, they made him wise unto salvation. Faith is the instrument of saving wisdom (Ephesians 2:8-9), and faith is a result of hearing the Word of God (Romans 10:17). It is imperative to instill scriptural truth into our children, for the Bible reveals the way of salvation. (See Proverbs 22:6.)

Verse 16. All Scripture is "inspired." The Greek word is *theopneustos,* made up of *theos* (God) and *pneustos*

169

(breath), thus literally meaning "God-breathed." "All" (*pas*) means that every part is inspired. God "breathed out" the Scriptures. He did not leave the human authors to their own ideas and limitations, but He guided and controlled them by the Holy Spirit (II Peter 1:21; John 14:26).

Paul apparently had the Old Testament primarily in mind when he wrote this verse. The New Testament was not completely written at the time, and it certainly was not gathered and organized as we know it today. Nevertheless, Paul had already quoted the Gospel of Luke as Scripture (I Timothy 5:18), and somewhere around this time Peter cited all of Paul's letters as Scripture (II Peter 3:15-16). God inspired the New Testament as surely as the Old.

The Word of God is profitable for "doctrine" (*didaskalia*, literally, teaching material). No doctrine that is not enunciated in Scripture should be imposed on the believer. Experience should never be an absolute criterion for establishing a doctrine. Experience must be subject to the teachings of Scripture, not vice versa. The Bible is not right because it parallels an experience; the experience is right because it parallels the Bible! Doctrine has to do with the nature of God, His relationship with humanity, redemption, the sanctified lifestyle, the last things, and eternal life. People may spout philosophy about any of those themes, but only what is written in the Book is to be taken as absolute truth. "Yea, let God be true, but every man a liar" (Romans 3:4).

"Reproof" is *elegmos,* "conviction." The Word may be wielded with such authority and force that it will evoke at least conviction, if not confession. Love does not exclude rebuke; verily, it includes it! The coming of the Holy

Spirit into people's lives is to be marked by reproof: "And when he [the Comforter] is come, he will reprove the world of sin, and of righteousness, and of judgment" (John 16:8). We are to "have no fellowship with the unfruitful works of darkness, but rather reprove them" (Ephesians 5:11). We ought not be timid in declaring the whole counsel of God!

"Correction" is *epanorthosis,* "restoration to an upright or right state." The Word of God furnishes us with a criterion, a plumbline, by which we measure doctrine and lifestyle.

"Instruction in righteousness" is *paideia,* literally, "training." Originating from *pais,* (child), it originally meant "the rearing of a child." Inherent in the word is discipline, something every child of God sorely needs (II Timothy 2:25; Ephesians 6:4; Hebrews 12:5, 11). We need to hear the word preached, have it explained, and see it enforced in the church. "In righteousness" stands in contrast to "rudiments of the world" (Colossians 2:20).

Verse 17. The purpose of all the training, discipline, correction, and instruction is to "perfect," or mature, the believer. In this way, he will be prepared, fitted, or equipped for "good works," or effectual service.

Footnotes

[1]Wuest, 146.
[2]Jamieson, Fausset, and Brown, 1232.
[3]*Liberty Bible Commentary,* 648.
[4]*Jamieson, Fausset, and Brown,* 1258.

II TIMOTHY
Chapter Four

VI. Paul's Final Charge (4:1-5)

A. Responsibility before God (4:1)

(1) I charge thee therefore before God, and the Lord Jesus Christ, who shall judge the quick and the dead at his appearing and his kingdom.

Verse 1. This verse begins Paul's final charge to Timothy. A charge goes beyond a commandment in that it carries with it a moral obligation to follow through in explicit obedience. Paul chose a Greek word used then for calling the pagan Greek gods to witness. He adjured Timothy by the Deity, intimating the seriousness with which the apostle spoke. Apostasy was rampant, believers were falling prey to false teachers, and the church was operating in dangerous times. Paul himself knew that his own time was short. It is easy to read the deep concern in these next few verses.

The rendering "God, and the Lord Jesus Christ" does not suggest that God and Jesus are two separate, distinct "persons" in the Godhead. The Greek text uses only one definite article before the two designations, clearly identifying God as Jesus. Wuest commented, "The expression 'God, and the Lord Jesus Christ' is in a construction in Greek which requires us to understand that the word 'God' and the names 'Lord Jesus Christ' refer to the same person. The translation should read, 'our God, even Christ Jesus.' "[1]

Jesus Christ is the one who shall appear, establish His kingdom, and judge the living and the dead at a future judgment. Jesus spoke of that time in John 5:28-29: "For the hour is coming, in the which all that are in the graves [the "dead"] shall hear his voice, and shall come forth." Those who are alive [the "quick"] and remain shall be "caught up together with them in the clouds, to meet the Lord in the air" (I Thessalonians 4:17). The rapture (catching away) itself will be a judgment (Revelation 20:6), to be followed by the "judgment seat of Christ" (Romans 14:10; II Corinthians 5:10), a judgment of the nations (Matthew 25:31-34), and the final White Throne judgment (Revelation 20:11-15).

B. Using the Word (4:2)

(2) Preach the word; be instant in season, out of season; reprove, rebuke, exhort with all longsuffering and doctrine.

Verse 2. The heart of the charge is given in the first three words: "Preach the word" The Greek word *kerusso* draws a picture, not of a clergyman holding forth from a lofty pulpit, but of the imperial herald. The herald proclaimed the announcements of the emperor in an authoritative tone and manner. He was usually rather formal and grave, commanding the respect and attention of all. Everyone listened to what was said because the message must be adhered to or obeyed. The imperial herald did not clown around. He was an ambassador on business. That was the image Paul wanted to conjure up in Timothy's mind. He wanted him to feel the heavy responsibility.

What are we to preach? "The word." The word is (1) the "good news" of the coming of the Messiah into the world—His life, teachings, death, burial, resurrection, ascension, and promised return. We are delivered from the law of sin and death (Romans 8:2). Our Kinsman has redeemed us. (2) It is the entire body of revealed truth, both in the Old Testament and the New Testament. The Old Testament word is "a schoolmaster" to bring us to Christ (Galatians 3:24). It is to be used to point people to Jesus, the promised Messiah (Acts 8:27-35). (3) It is, in a sense, Christ Himself, the living Word (John 1:1, 14). To the Corinthians Paul said, "For I determined not to know any thing among you, save Jesus Christ, and him crucified. . . . And my speech and my preaching was not with enticing words of man's wisdom, but in demonstration of the Spirit and of power: that your faith should not stand in the wisdom of men, but in the power of God" (I Corinthians 2:2, 4-5). People's philosophies, book reviews, politics, current events, economics, and other popular interests usually have little to do with the Word. The herald does not choose his pronouncements—the Emperor dictates that! If that dictation is not acceptable to him, he should relinquish his status as a preacher!

The minister is to be always ready to proclaim the message. "Instant" is *epistemi,* meaning "to stand by in readiness." "In season, out of season" is *eukairos, akairos,* meaning "opportune, inopportune." He is to be prepared to deliver the Word when it seems propitious and at times when it does not. Preachers do not always

175

set the stage themselves; sometimes God makes the arrangements.

Our preaching is to include rebuke (censure, admonition) and reproof (correction, conviction). That alone may seem harsh, but it is to be tempered with exhortation (comfort, encouragement), longsuffering (patience), and doctrine (instruction, teaching). Doctrine is to be the basis for reproof, not the minister's personal feelings. There must be a mingling of severity and gentleness. Love does not mean extending liberty without limits, nor is harshness a motivator to true righteousness.

C. Warning of Apostasy (4:3-4)

(3) For the time will come when they will not endure sound doctrine; but after their own lusts shall they heap to themselves teachers, having itching ears; (4) and they shall turn away their ears from the truth, and shall be turned unto fables.

*Verse 3.*The time described in this verse has come! Such attitudes abound in our day. Many people, even professing Christians, do not want doctrinal instruction. The "itching ears" of the carnal seek a compromising preacher who will scratch them, who will justify and condone the fulfillment of their lusts. Somewhere a person can find a teacher who will say things just the way he wants!

Compromise is an ugly word when it involves the surrender of biblical principles in order to appease the masses. Some, for the sake of number, or prestige, or social acceptance, have abandoned elements of the gospel that are least liked by those governed by carnal appetites. Modernists have surrendered new-birth salvation for easy

believism, absolute truth for relativism, scriptural principles for situational ethics. Instead of the sinfulness of
humanity, they extol the divinity of humanity. For crea-
tionism they proffer atheistic evolution. For baptism they
sprinkle. For Holy Spirit infilling they substitute confir-
mation. For humility they bestow the gratification of
pride. For holiness they offer excuses. Acts 2:38 salvation is still the ticket to ride the heaven-bound train.
Millions will be left standing at the station, surprised and
aghast that they were ill informed or that they did not
take God's Word at face value.

Such persons desire many teachers—"heap" (*episo-
reuo*, to accumulate in piles). They go from one to the
other until they find one exactly to their liking. But even
those relationships are often short-lived. Variety delights
itching ears. As Bengel said, "He who despises sound
teaching, leaves sound teaching; they seek instructors like
themselves."

Verse 4. These hearers will "turn away," or position
themselves where they will not hear the truth. It is
righteous retribution that when people turn away from
the truth they turn to fables. (See Jeremiah 2:19.) It is
amazing what some people will believe once they have
decided against the truth. What perverted tastes can be
developed by those who fail to receive a "love of the
truth"; God sends "strong delusion" their way (II Thessalonians 2:10-11)! Someone has observed, "Those who
reject the truth are abandoned by the just judgment to
credit the most degrading nonsense."

"Shall be turned" is *ektrepo*, a medical term meaning "to twist out of place." We can picture a dislocated
arm, wrenched out of place, hanging uselessly by one's

177

side. It is a sad sight indeed to see once-solid saints "twisted out of place" by the guile of sweet deception. It can happen to anyone who fails to keep his desires in check and his feet firmly planted on absolute truth.

D. Faithfulness in Ministry (4:5)

(5) But watch thou in all things, endure afflictions, do the work of an evangelist, make full proof of thy ministry.

Verse 5. "But" is in contrast to the ear-ticklers mentioned in verse 3. Regardless of what others are doing, we must be watchful—spiritually alert and sober in all circumstances. The admonition to "endure afflictions" means that we must not run when problems arise or when we encounter opposition. (See also 2:3.)

"The work of an evangelist" is soulwinning. An evangelist carries the gospel to persons and places previously untouched by the gospel. The minister must not forget this first love. Nothing will keep a preacher fresh in the Spirit like reaching out to the untouched. When counseling and administration become weighty, let him carry a witness to a lost person. Seeing the impact of the gospel on virgin soil is truly refreshing. The pastor must not forget, although he may have many administrative duties, that he is still a missionary pastor.

Faithfulness to be watchful, endure afflictions, and evangelize helps a preacher "make full proof of" (*plerophoreo,* to fully perform) of his ministry. His service and spiritual activities need to be well-rounded and full-orbed, lacking nothing. (See Acts 12:25; Romans 15:19; Colossians 4:17.)

VII. Paul's Final Testimony (4:6-8)

A. His Readiness To Depart This Life (4:6)
(6) For I am now ready to be offered, and the time of my departure is at hand.

Verse 6. A literal rendering from the Greek is, "I am already being poured out," indicating that Paul truly saw himself as a libation being poured out upon the sacrifice. He was fully prepared to be sacrificed for the cause of Christ. Apparently the sentence of death had been passed upon him. It is interesting to note that Peter also knew when his time was near (II Peter 1:14).

What a wonderful feeling it must be to come to the end of life with a readiness that almost welcomes the blade! Paul had said to the Philippians, "So now also Christ shall be magnified in my body, whether it be by life, or by death. For to me to live is Christ, and to die is gain. But if I live in the flesh, this is the fruit of my labour: yet what I shall choose I wot not. For I am in a strait betwixt two, having a desire to depart, and to be with Christ: which is far better: nevertheless to abide in the flesh is more needful for you" (Philippians 1:20-24).

Paul perhaps used the libation metaphor more easily since he knew that he would suffer decapitation rather than crucifixion. Roman citizens were not crucified; the death sentence for them was usually carried out by beheading.

It is interesting that Paul used *analuo* for "departure." While it was a fairly common euphemism for death, it was mostly used in military terminology as when a soldier takes down his tent and moves on, or when a ship

179

hoists anchor in preparation for sailing. Paul was saying, "Anchors aweigh, my boy! It is time for me to sail on!"

B. His Record of Spiritual
Accomplishments (4:7)

(7) I have fought a good fight, I have finished my course, I have kept the faith.

Verse 7. This trinity of testimonies constitutes one of the best-loved and most-quoted verses in the Bible. Everyone would like a witness like this when they come to die!

In this brief glance backward over his storied life, Paul used the figures of a Greek wrestler, a Greek runner, and a Roman soldier. In the first, he used the definite article before "fight" so that he does not appear to be egotistical. He was saying, "I have spent my life in the good fight of faith." "Fight" is *agon,* used of Greek athletic contests. "Have fought" is *agonizomai* in the perfect tense. It speaks of an action completed in the past with present results. He had struggled to a finish against sin. He had not eradicated it, but he had not lost the battle in his own life. He had no regrets. It was a "good" fight. It was worthwhile. It had not been joy all the way, but joy all along the way. If he had it to do over, he would do it again. He had practiced what he had earlier preached to Timothy: "Fight the good fight of faith, lay hold on eternal life" (I Timothy 6:12).

The "course," *dromos,* was a racecourse, much like the modern stadium courses with lanes drawn for the runners. He had finished his prescribed distance and had crossed the finish line. He had not quit. He had completed the marathon. He had outdistanced all his competitors.

"The faith" is the deposit of truth placed in his keeping. The word "kept" is *tereo,* "to keep by guarding." As a soldier would stand guard over a particular treasure, he had guarded the integrity of the faith. It would be intact when he met the Captain. He had braved the onslaught of the Judaizers, the proto-Gnostics, the philosophers, the heathen, the Romans, and "the beasts of Ephesus." He held on tenaciously, even when he was at the whipping post, under a pile of rocks at Lystra, in dank prisons, standing before rulers, or clinging to a piece of broken ship in the sea. He never lost the faith!

C. His Anticipation of Eternal Life (4:8)

(8) Henceforth there is laid up for me a crown of righteousness, which the Lord, the righteous judge, shall give me at that day: and not to me only, but unto all them also that love his appearing.

Verse 8. "Henceforth" means "because of the truth of the foregoing testimony." He anticipated the victor's "crown"—*stephanos,* a laurel wreath of ivy or oak leaves placed on the head of the winner in the athletic games. We do not have it now, in this life, for here we are but heirs. But "in that day" we shall have it in possession!

Paul called the Lord "the righteous judge" because he had found Him to always be fair in his dealings, impartial in his judgments, and a magistrate who never made a mistake. He saw Him as an umpire who never made a bad call, a referee who had an all-seeing eye. Beyond salvation itself Paul would receive no reward that he had not labored for by God's grace, but he would be denied nothing that was due him based on God's promises.

This award is available to all Christians. To "love the appearing" of the Lord would be to have our affections set on things above (Colossians 3:2), our first love firmly fixed on the one who "cometh with clouds" (Revelation 1:7). Adam, after he had sinned, did not want the Lord to visit him in the garden, as had been His practice (Genesis 3:8). He was guilty. He was naked. He was unprepared for fellowship. When God came, Adam hid himself—"I was afraid . . . and I hid myself" (Genesis 3:10). He would have preferred the Lord to have delayed His coming. By contrast, John appealed as he stood on the hot sands of Patmos, "Even so, come, Lord Jesus" (Revelation 22:20). The difference was that one had become guilty before God, with outstanding sin in his life, but the other had been forgiven and cleansed and stood eager to meet his Redeemer.

How important it is to love, long for, and anticipate His appearing! "For the Lord himself shall descend from heaven with a shout, with the voice of the archangel, and with the trump of God: and the dead in Christ shall rise first: then we which are alive and remain shall be caught up together with them in the clouds, to meet the Lord in the air: and so shall we ever be with the Lord. Wherefore comfort one another with these words" (I Thessalonians 4:16-18).

With this great crescendo of faith-filled expression, Paul concluded his epistle except for his personal remarks. What a tremendous attitude for one who was incarcerated in a musty Roman jail awaiting execution on trumped-up charges! He could have been bitter. He could easily have hated, but he knew a better way of handling the situation. He loved when he could have despised his accusers. His attitude was a magnificent display of the real spirit of Christianity. As the songwriter sang his prayer:

> *Show me thy way, O Lord,*
> *Show me thy way, O Lord.*
> *Let me love when I'm hated,*
> *Spread joy unabated,*
> *Show me thy way, O Lord.*

VIII. Paul's Final Instructions (4:9-15)

A. For Timothy To Join Him in Rome (4:9-12)
(9) Do thy diligence to come shortly unto me; (10) for Demas hath forsaken me, having loved this present world, and is departed unto Thessalonica; Crescens to Galatia, Titus unto Dalmatia. (11) Only Luke is with me. Take Mark, and bring him with thee: for he is profitable to me for the ministry. (12) And Tychicus have I sent to Ephesus.

Verse 9. "Do thy diligence" is from the same Greek word translated as "study" in 2:15. It means "do your best." We do not know whether Timothy reached Paul before his death.

Why this pressing invitation? Timothy would be a comfort to Paul, and Paul would encourage and strengthen Timothy to carry on the work after he was gone.

Verse 10. Paul was running out of friends: "Demas hath forsaken me." Demas had evidently been one of the apostle's trusted friends and co-workers. Paul had called him "my fellowlabourer" (Philemon 24), and Demas was with him in Rome when he wrote to the Colossians (Colos-

183

sians 4:14). But Demas had let his mentor down. He decided that he no longer wanted to walk with Paul. He chose to return to the "world," where rules "the lust of the flesh, and the lust of the eyes, and the pride of life" (I John 2:16). Perhaps he merely wanted to live with a greater degree of safety, or comfort, or acceptance. The "world" has many allurements, not all of which are clothed with immorality. Greed has a potent magnetism. Jealousy, rivalries, witchcraft, heresies, and all the other works of the flesh sing a sweet siren's song (Galatians 5:19-21). All that is in opposition to righteousness is of the world.

We must forever leave behind the things of the world and the thinking of the world. If we harbor a love and a longing for those things from which we have been delivered, there will be opportunity to return to them (Hebrews 11:15). But backsliding is like a dog returning to its vomit and a sow to her wallowing in the mire (II Peter 2:22). "Remember Lot's wife" (Luke 17:32).

Not only had Demas left the party, but Crescens had gone to Galatia in Asia Minor, and Titus had departed for Dalmatia on the eastern shore of the Adriatic Sea north of Macedonia. This statement reveals that Titus had completed his mission in Crete and had since been with Paul in Rome. These personal attendants were not now with him, but he evidently still had friends in Rome who visited him (verse 21) but who had not stood with him during his trial (verse 16).

Verse 11. Luke was the only person staying with Paul at this time. Paul called him "the beloved physician" (Colossians 4:14), and he seemed to be a consistent companion of the apostle. He probably was Paul's personal secretary at this time and the one who took the dictation of this particular epistle.

Mark was the same disciple who had once deserted Paul and over whom Paul and Barnabas had a disagreement (Acts 13:13; 15:36-41). Mark had subsequently proven himself faithful and was in Paul's good graces again. Here he received the apostle's highest accolade: "He is profitable to me." Apparently, he was now very close to Paul, for Paul wanted him to come with Timothy.

Verse 12. Tychicus hailed from the province of Asia and was with Paul on his last journey to Jerusalem (Acts 20:4). He served as a courier, carrying the letters to the Colossians (4:7-8) and to the Ephesians (6:21). Esteemed by Paul, he was called a beloved brother, a faithful minister, and a fellow servant in the Lord." Since Timothy was evidently in Ephesus at the time of the writing, Tychicus may have been the bearer of this epistle to Timothy. He would likely have been sent to relieve Timothy as supervisor of the work there.

B. Bring Some Important Items (4:13)

(13) The cloke that I left at Troas with Carpus, when thou comest, bring with thee, and the books, but especially the parchments.

Verse 13. The cloak was a knee-length cape with a hole for the neck. It would be valuable to Paul during his imprisonment in the long Italian winter. Such cloaks were made of goat's hair, with which Paul was familiar, knowing the tent-making trade. Of Carpus, with whom Paul had left the cloak, nothing more is known. Evidently he was a trusted friend. Troas was a port city on the north-

185

west coast of Asia Minor between Ephesus and Macedonia.

The "books" (*biblia*, papers, written documents, from which we get "Bible") were scrolls made from papyrus. The pith of the papyrus plant, which grew along the Nile River, was cut in strips and laid in rows, with other layers of rows crossing them, and then the whole was pressed into a paperlike material called papyrus. Many ancient documents were of papyrus, probably including many original manuscripts of books of the Bible.

The "parchments" (*membrana*, animal skins, usually skins of goats or sheep, from which we derive "membrane") seemed to be of great concern to Paul; he used the word "especially." Parchment material was much more expensive than papyrus and was used for those documents that were of greater importance, since it was more durable than papyrus.

What was written in these books and parchments? It is very possible that they were Paul's own writings. Or they could have been his personal copies of the Hebrew Scriptures. He undoubtedly kept these close at hand at all times. He had told Timothy to "give attendance to reading" (I Timothy 4:13), and certainly he did himself.

It is interesting to note that William Tyndale, who first translated the New Testament into English, was also desirous of his books during his long imprisonment near Brussels. In 1536, while in Vilvorde Castle, he implored the governor to provide warmer clothing, a woolen shirt, and above all, his Hebrew Bible, grammar, and dictionary. What comfort the Holy Writ can be, especially in one's lonely and trying moments!

C. Beware of Alexander (4:14-15)

(14) Alexander the coppersmith did me much evil: the Lord reward him according to his works: (15) of whom be thou ware also; for he hath greatly withstood our words.

Verse 14. Since Alexander was such a common name, Paul identified him more specifically as "the coppersmith." No doubt Timothy understood exactly who he was. He may have been the Alexander of Ephesus mentioned in Acts 19:33 or the man excommunicated in I Timothy 1:20. Ultimately, the Lord will reward such a person for his misdeeds, so Paul left the situation in His hands. But future judgment does not preclude present discipline (I Timothy 1:20). The church disciplined him as an erring brother, if indeed he was the one excommunicated in I Timothy 1:20.

Verse 15. Whoever Alexander was, he had abused or opposed Paul in some way, probably by putting up arguments against his authority or his teachings. Paul was not trying to slander an individual but merely issued a warning to Timothy that he should beware lest he also be troubled by him. Paul similarly told the Thessalonians to "know them which labour among you" (I Thessalonians 5:12). Such reporting saves the body of Christ much hurt and embarrassment.

IX. Paul's Final Report (4:16-18)

A. His Lonely Defense before the Roman Court (4:16)

(16) At my first answer no man stood with me, but all men forsook me: I pray God that it may not be laid to their charge.

Verse 16. Paul's "first answer" was his first defense of himself before Nero's tribunal. The Greek word is *apologia,* a technical word used in the law courts to describe one's verbal defense of himself before his accusers.

Paul stood alone, forsaken. He used the same word when he reported, "Demas hath forsaken me" (verse 10). Those who should have been by his side were not. It must have been a lonely time for the courageous apostle. In their behalf, however, we should note that Nero had initiated a most severe persecution of Christians, blaming the burning of Rome on them. The evidence points to Nero himself as having set the conflagration in order to redesign the city according to his wishes and blame the Christians for the damage. He had many of them wrapped in clothing soaked in pitch, impaled upon stakes, and set on fire, thus using them to light the course at the Circus Maximus so that the games could proceed at night.

Paul's magnanimous spirit is always in evidence—"I pray God that it may not be laid to their charge." Did he first hear this prayer falling from the lips of Stephen? (Acts 7:60). Jesus had set the pattern for them both (Luke 23:34). Forgiveness is the alternative to bitterness.

B. His Divine Counsel (4:17)

(17) Notwithstanding the Lord stood with me, and strengthened me; that by me the preaching might be fully known, and that all the Gentiles might hear: and I was delivered out of the mouth of the lion.

Verse 17. When all others fail and forsake, the Lord will be there. He will not leave us or forsake us (Joshua

1:5; Matthew 28:20; Hebrews 13:5). He was present to strengthen the apostle as he made his lonely defense.

Paul's ministry was not limited to the pulpit—he could preach in court as well as in church. His mouth was filled with the words that had been in his heart. He had a hearing before the imperial court. How else could the gospel have penetrated the upper echelons of Roman government had not Paul been the subject of persecution? He saw it all from the perspective of his ministry: "that the Gentiles might hear."

From this passage we might deduce that his defense was before Nero himself. Without a doubt, he held nothing back and was as bold as he had been before Felix. By his preaching the message was "fully known." How exciting today when we are given the opportunity to present the gospel in circles once thought impenetrable! Everyone should have the chance to hear the gospel story.

"The mouth of the lion" is probably a figure of speech showing that Paul had been spared, albeit temporarily, from imminent danger. It did not refer to the lions in the arena, for Roman citizens did not suffer that form of execution. Perhaps it is a reference to the emperor himself. Some commentators see it as an allusion to Psalm 22:21. At any rate, Paul had been spared for sufficient time to write this beautiful farewell epistle.

C. His Confidence of Future Assistance (4:18)

(18) And the Lord shall deliver me from every evil work, and will preserve me unto his heavenly kingdom: to whom be glory for ever and ever. Amen.

Verse 18. Paul's faith encompassed the past, present, and the future. "[God] delivered us . . . and doth deliver . . . will yet deliver" (II Corinthians 1:10). He has never stopped delivering. What He has done, He will do today as it pleases Him! Paul knew that he faced death, but whether he lived or died, he knew that God would grant him spiritual victory.

"Every evil work" includes every design upon our souls by the devil—every temptation, every nefarious strategy, every wicked enticement—and even those dark possibilities within our own hearts. Divine preservation is a common theme in Paul's writings (II Timothy 1:12; 3:11; Romans 8:38-39; Ephesians 1:13; 4:30).

"To whom be glory. . . ." Paul seemed to be compelled to stop and praise the Lord for the hope engendered by the foregoing statement.

X. Paul's Final Greetings and Farewell (4:19-22)

A. Salutation to Friends (4:19)
(19) Salute Prisca and Aquila, and the household of Onesiphorus.

Verse 19. In these last greetings, Paul revealed his deep concern for people. He wanted them to know that in his last moments he remembered them and their service both to him and the Lord.

Prisca (Priscilla) and Aquila were the friends of Paul with whom he had labored in Corinth (Acts 18:1-2; I Corinthians 16:19) and who had won Apollos to the Lord in Ephesus (Acts 18:24-28). Onesiphorus was discussed in II Timothy 1:16. He was probably dead by this time, but his memory lingered in Paul's mind, and Paul sent greetings to his family who still remained at Ephesus.

B. Information about Friends (4:20)
(20) Erastus abode at Corinth: but Trophimus have I left at Miletum sick.

Verse 20. Erastus, who had earlier been sent with Timothy on a mission to Macedonia (Acts 19:22), had returned and stayed at Corinth, his home town. From Romans 16:23 we learn that he had been the city treasurer there.

Trophimus had been left sick at Miletum. Even the apostles did not have the power to heal at will. They prayed for healing, anointing with oil (James 5:14-16), but the healing was done by God alone. He does not always heal instantaneously or as we desire. The realities of life are with us until we are clothed with a new body (I Corinthians 15:51-54; II Corinthians 5:2). The Miletum mentioned here was probably Miletus of Ionia, which is near Ephesus.

C. Salutation from Friends (4:21)
(21) Do thy diligence to come before winter. Eubulus greeteth thee, and Pudens, and Linus, and Claudia, and all the brethren.

Verse 21. Paul wanted Timothy to come to Rome "before winter." One reason may have been because he knew his time was short. Another reason was surely that sailing in the winter was a most dangerous proposition. Moreover, Paul would need his cloak before that time.

Nothing else is known of the last four names mentioned by Paul. While no positive identifications can be made, there is strong indication in extrabiblical writings that Pudens and Claudia later married—he having been a Roman knight and she a Briton.

Having mentioned the names that came easily to mind, Paul did not wish to overlook anyone: "and all the brethren."

D. Benediction (4:22)

(22) The Lord Jesus Christ be with thy spirit. Grace be with you. Amen.

Verse 22. The epistle fittingly concludes with a benediction—a prayer that Christ would abide "with thy spirit," enlightening, strengthening, and renewing.

"Grace be with you." If grace can save, it can keep. It can keep us humble. It can put a crown of glory on our heads in the hereafter. The "you" is plural, indicating that Paul included all those who were with Timothy in Ephesus.

"Amen"—so be it!

Footnote
[1]Wuest, 152.

THE EPISTLE OF
PAUL THE APOSTLE TO

TITUS

Introduction to Titus

The Author
The apostle Paul is the author of this letter (1:1). (See the General Introduction.)

The Recipient
The second of Paul's pastoral epistles is addressed to Titus, one of his converts (1:4). Titus, a Greek, accompanied his spiritual mentor to Jerusalem when Paul visited the leaders there to discuss his doctrinal positions. The demand by Jewish Christians for his circumcision was strong but was successfully resisted (Galatians 2:1-5). This test case was a great victory for the gospel of Christ, establishing the church's position as a separate entity from Judaism.

Titus was a trusted co-laborer and sometimes served as a courier for the epistles of Paul. At some point, he was assigned to oversee the young church that had been established on the island of Crete. The island of Crete is southeast of mainland, Greece. It is approximately 150 miles long and 35 miles wide, making it the fourth largest island in the Mediterranean Sea.

Titus was to stay on Crete until his replacement arrived (3:12) and then meet Paul in Nicopolis on the west coast of Greece. Paul also sent Titus to Corinth to help correct some disorders there and initiate an offering for the poor saints at Jerusalem (II Corinthians 8:6, 16-24). Judging by Paul's remarks about him, Titus evidently did a commendable job in working through the thorny problems in Corinth (II Corinthians 2:13; 8:23; 12:18).

The last we read of Titus, he was evidently sent on a mission to Dalmatia (in modern Yugoslavia) (II Timothy 4:10). Considering these assignments, he was obviously a capable and resourceful leader.

The Church

The origin of the church on Crete is unknown, but it may have been founded by Cretan Jews returning from Jerusalem after Pentecost (Acts 2:11). Paul apparently labored on Crete after his first Roman imprisonment, probably with Titus by his side (Titus 1:5). When he left, he commissioned Titus to remain there as an overseeing elder.

Place and Date of Writing

This epistle was written about the same time as I Timothy, between Paul's first and second Roman imprisonment, probably around A.D. 63-65. He was possibly in Corinth when he penned the letter.

Emphasis

In his writings to Timothy, Paul focused on *doctrine*. To Titus he emphasized *duty*. What was to be *protected* in I Timothy and *proclaimed* in II Timothy was to be *practiced* in Titus. Paul consistently admonished the Cretans to good works (1:16; 2:7, 14; 3:1, 8, 14).

Some outstanding summaries of fundamental Christian doctrines are found in 1:1-3; 2:11-14; and 3:4-7.

Outline of Titus

I. Salutation (1:1-4)
   A. The Author (1:1-3)
   B. The Recipient (1:4a)
   C. The Greeting (1:4b)

II. Instructions Concerning Elders (1:5-9)
   A. Personal Responsibility of Titus (1:5)
   B. Qualifications for Elders (1:6-9)

III. Duties of the Elders (1:10-16)
   A. To Identify and Silence False Teachers (1:10-11)
   B. To Rebuke the Spiritual Sluggards (1:12-16)

IV. Instructions to Various Groups in the Church (2:1-10)
   A. The Older Men (2:1-2)
   B. The Older Women (2:3)
   C. The Younger Women (2:4-5)
   D. The Younger Men (2:6-8)
   E. The Servants (2:9-10)

V. The Motivation for Committed Christian Living (2:11-15)

    A. The Appearance of God's Grace (2:11)
    B. The Teaching of God's Grace (2:12-13)
    C. The Effects of God's Grace (2:14)
    D. The Continuity of God's Grace (2:15)

VI. Responsibilities of the Church (3:1-11)
    A. To Be Subject to Authorities (3:1)
    B. To Show Brotherly Kindness (3:2)
    C. To Give Because We Have Received (3:3-7)
    D. To Maintain Good Works (3:8)
    E. To Avoid Useless Controversies and Contentions (3:9)
    F. To Reject Divisive Persons (3:10-11)

VII. Conclusion (3:12-15)
    A. Replacements for Titus (3:12)
    B. Assistance for Workers on Their Journey (3:13-14)
    C. Benediction (3:15)

TITUS
Chapter One

I. Salutation (1:1-4)

A. The Author (1:1-3)
(1) Paul, a servant of God, and an apostle of Jesus Christ, according to the faith of God's elect, and the acknowledging of the truth which is after godliness; (2) in hope of eternal life, which God, that cannot lie, promised before the world began; (3) but hath in due times manifested his word through preaching, which is committed unto me according to the commandment of God our Saviour.

Verse 1. Paul identified himself as a servant (*doulos,* slave) and an apostle. "According to the faith of God's elect" means that his apostleship was in harmony with the revelation of Jesus Christ to which the elect have committed themselves. The knowledge and faith of God's people was in accord with Paul's apostleship; that is, true believers have no problem with his authority and credentials. Those who question his standing reveal their own lack of spiritual understanding and discernment.

"God's elect" refers to those who are born again, keeping the faith, and living a victorious, overcoming life. They are viewed here as a group, an entity, a body rather than as individuals. God predestined the elect (Ephesians 1:4-5; II Timothy 1:9) to eternal life. He does not select people unilaterally without regard to human will. God never violates the human right of choice as a moral agent. Our induction into the number of "the elect" is based on our personal faith and obedience to the gospel.

Paul's apostleship was also in accordance with "the acknowledging of the truth which is after godliness." It was in agreement with absolute truth, not some spurious theory or philosophy that exists to serve its own ends, but the gospel that was "at the first . . spoken by the Lord, and was confirmed unto us by them that heard him" (Hebrews 2:3).

Godliness and truth are inextricably linked. Truth naturally produces godliness. The theories and doctrines of modern philosophers lead to irreverence, pride, idolatry and self-justified ungodliness. Truth points to the way of escape from carnal reasoning, selfishness, and insincerity. To acknowledge truth is to envision the means to live above reproach.

Verse 2. Paul indicated that his apostolic service was in hope of eternal life, which God has promised. The promise was in the past, the basis for it is in the present power of the gospel, and the eternal life is yet future. Eternal life is a future reality; we have it within us now in seed form (John 3:36; I John 5:11-12).

We yet struggle with this present existence (Romans 8:19-23). "We are saved by hope: but hope that is seen is not hope: for what a man seeth, why doth he yet hope for? But if we hope for that we see not [redemption of the body, i. e., eternal life (verse 23)], then do we with patience wait for it" (Romans 8:24-25).

"Before the world began" indicates a decision that God made even before the creation of humanity. It was not revealed until a time foreordained—"in due times" (verse 3). Some commentators suggest that the phrase in verse 2 means "from ancient times." Some trinitarians suggest that the Father spoke this promise to the "eternal Son," but there is no scriptural basis for a preexistent Son, except in the redemptive plan of God (John 1:1-14; Hebrews 1:1-8).

The verse emphasizes that God cannot lie to show that the promise of eternal life is an absolutely certain hope.

Verse 3. The birth, life, death, resurrection, and ascension of Christ took place at the precise moments in history foreordained by God. Paul referred to such specificity on numerous occasions (Romans 5:6; Galatians 4:4; Ephesians 1:10). God left nothing to chance. "In due times" reminds us that God has a clear overview of time and eternity and will orchestrate future events just as He has throughout history.

"His word" is the gospel, in which the promise of eternal life is embodied. This word, or revealed will of God, is announced through the medium of preaching, or more literally, "heralding." It is this responsibility that was committed to Paul, and such commitment formed the basis of His apostleship. Paul was constantly aware of this calling and referred to it throughout his writings.

The term "God our Saviour" also appears freely in Paul's epistles—he employed "Saviour" in reference to God six times in the Pastoral Epistles (I Timothy 1:1; 2:3; 4:10; Titus 1:3; 2:10; 3:4). Jude 25 refers to "the only wise God our Saviour," and Luke 1:47 quotes Mary as calling God her Savior. Titus 1:4 says Jesus is our Savior.

There is no contradiction here. God is one Spirit (John 4:24; Ephesians 4:4). He manifested Himself in the Son by the Incarnation. God became our Savior by coming in the flesh as Jesus Christ. Since there is only one God (I Timothy 2:5), there is only one Savior (Isaiah 43:11). The term "God our Savior" is appropriate because Jesus is God the Father manifested in the flesh to be our Savior. (See Matthew 1:21, 23; John 10:30; 14:6-11; I Timothy 3:16.)

B. The Recipient (1:4a)
(4a) To Titus, mine own son after the common faith.

Verse 4a. Paul addressed the epistle to Titus, claiming him as his "son in the faith." Apparently Paul was instrumental in Titus's conversion and development as a Christian. Titus became one of Paul's personal emissaries (II Corinthians 8:6) and faithfully labored with him, proclaiming "the common faith."

C. The Greeting (1:4b)
(4b) Grace, mercy, and peace, from God the Father and the Lord Jesus Christ our Saviour.

Verse 4b. The apostle invoked the peace, mercy, and grace of God upon his co-worker, again employing the term "Saviour," only this time calling the Lord Jesus Christ our Savior. As we have seen, there is no conflict between verse 3 and verse 4. The double usage of "Saviour" is clear evidence of the absolute deity of Jesus Christ. (For further discussion of this greeting phrase, see the commentary on I Timothy 1:1-2).

II. Instructions Concerning Elders (1:5-9)

A. Personal Responsibility of Titus (1:5)

(5) For this cause left I thee in Crete, that thou shouldest set in order the things that are wanting, and ordain elders in every city, as I had appointed thee.

Verse 5. Paul got quickly to the business at hand, reminding Titus of his mission in Crete. Titus was there by Paul's authority, having been appointed to certain tasks. Crete was a long, narrow island in the Mediterranean Sea and probably the original home of the Philistines. Its cities or population centers were few, but it appears that there were at least several Christian communities existing in them. The use of the word *apoleipo* (to leave behind temporarily) instead of *kataleipo* (to leave behind permanently) indicates that Titus was there on a temporary rather than permanent assignment.

It seems that the two men had worked together in Crete for a time, but Paul left before their work was finished. There were tasks left undone (*ta leiponta*). Titus was to straighten out (*epidiorthoo*) or stabilize the situation by appointing elders (presbyters) to oversee the local work of the churches. These were to be preaching elders (verse 9) charged with exhorting those who contradicted the truth and righting what they had wronged (verses 9-11). Evidently Christianity had been operative on the island long enough to develop qualified Christians and also to develop injurious irregularities.

It was likely that Paul had related these things to Titus orally and now sent this letter to verify Titus's authority as well as to remind him of his task.

B. Qualifications of Elders (1:6-9)

(6) If any be blameless, the husband of one wife, having faithful children not accused of riot or unruly. (7) For a bishop must be blameless, as the steward of God; not selfwilled, not soon angry, not given to wine, no striker, not given to filthy lucre; (8) but a lover of hospitality, a lover of good men, sober, just, holy, temperate; (9) holding fast the faithful word as he hath been taught, that he may be able by sound doctrine both to exhort and to convince the gainsayers.

Verse 6. An elder must meet certain qualifications. The first criterion is being blameless (*anegkletos*), indicating that no justifiable charge could be brought against his character. Second, he can have only one wife, a status also required in I Timothy. (For further discussion, see the commentary on I Timothy 3:2).

"Faithful children" means that the children of his household should be believers. They must certainly not be riotous (*asotia*, a profligate life) or unruly (*anupotaktos*, not subject to control) which would reflect negatively on the father's example or attitude in correction. A father cannot make his children love God, but as long as they live in his house he can require them to be respectful and obedient.

Verse 7. The church leader must be one against whom no serious accusation can be brought, particularly in the areas of morality and doctrine. He is a "steward" (*oikonomos*, which comes from words meaning "law of the house") of God—one who is charged with the care of another's possessions. As Hiebert said, "Because of his position he is a manager or administrator of God's house, dispensing under God to the members of the household the mysteries of God (I Cor. 4:1) and His manifold grace (I Peter 4:10)."[1]

To be self-willed is to seek first one's own pleasure. Hedonism was perhaps as rampant in Paul's day as in ours. The Christian leader has to be others-minded. "God is first; others are second; I am third."

"Not soon angry" corresponds to James 1:19—"slow to wrath." Self-control is to mark the life of the elder.

"Not given to wine" indicates that Christian leadership is limited to teetotallers. *Me paroinos* literally means "not alongside of wine" (as one rendered petulant by wine). Wine and other alcoholic beverages have no place in the lives of those who are pointing others to Christ and righteousness.

On "no striker" and "not given to filthy lucre" see the commentary on I Timothy 3:3.

Verse 8. On the requirements of "a lover of hospitality" and "sober," see the commentary on I Timothy 3:2.

"A lover of good men" (*philagathon*) is literally "a lover of goodness, or what is good." It can refer to people or things.

"Just" means "upright, reliable, trustworthy, fair-minded, impartial."

"Holy" (*hosios*) brings to mind a sense of piety, devotion, separation unto God.

"Temperate" (*egkrate,* having power over) means "self-controlled," not too far one way or the other, not extreme. This virtue is part of the fruit of the Spirit in Galatians 5:23.

Verse 9. The elder must be sound in the faith— "holding fast the faithful word." He must be characterized by doctrinal stability. He has withstood the opposition of the world and the flesh. He has maintained his stand for truth. He remains true to the faith in the midst of a crooked and perverse generation. "As he has been taught" means the teaching that came down from the apostles.

Gainsayers (*antilego*) are those who contradict or speak against what is right. Such people can only be turned around by those who are "able by sound doctrine both to exhort and to convince."

III. Duties of the Elders (1:10-16)

A. To Identify and Silence
False Teachers (1:10-11)

(10) For there are many unruly and vain talkers and deceivers, specially they of the circumcision: (11) whose mouths must be stopped, who subvert whole houses, teaching things which they ought not, for filthy lucre's sake.

Verses 10. The qualifications of a teaching elder include the ability to confute those who are glib speakers but devoid of truth and those who seek to deceive. Paul especially emphasized the undermining work of the Judaizers, who insisted that Christians were obligated to keep the law.

Verse 11. False teachers of this kind should be stopped and no forum afforded them to speak their empty and subversive words. The church in Thyatira was rebuked for tolerating "that woman Jezebel, which calleth herself a prophetess, to teach and seduce my servants" (Revelation 2:20). If false teachers are allowed to present their views, the chance is good that they will influence some of their hearers. On Crete, whole households had been affected. Entire families were upset and moved away from the truth faith. Thus such teachers must be silenced. The word used here literally means "to put something in their mouths" and was used of bridles and muzzles. We must give them no platform, overcome their rantings with absolute truths, and guard our pulpits.

The implication is that such people are often motivated by financial considerations. Mercenary motives can certainly be a driving force, sometimes surpassing religious zeal. Evidently in Crete these false prophets obtained money from the deceived families.

With "filthy lucre" as a goal, such teachers become very accommodating to the tastes of those involved. Base gain has a way of evoking compromise like nothing else. For this reason Christian ministers should never entertain impure motives or employ trickery in presenting the gospel. "For the appeal we make does not spring from error or impure motives, nor are we trying to trick you. . . . We are not trying to please men, but God. . . . You know we never used flattery, nor did we put on a mask to cover up greed. . . . We were not looking for praise from men, not from you or anyone else" (I Thessalonians 2:3-6, NIV). It is imperative that we preach with pure motives and use appropriate methods.

We should insist on the qualifications submitted in these verses when choosing Christian leaders today. Hiebert asked: "Are we insisting strongly enough on these qualifications for our ministers? Do we refuse men who do not have them? In admitting a man to the ministry, the primary consideration must ever be the integrity of

The Pastoral Epistles

his character rather than his spectacular gifts."² As it has
been said, "No intellectual power or pulpit brilliancy can
atone for the lack of solid Christian virtues and a blameless life."

B. To Rebuke the Spiritual Sluggards (1:12-16)

*(12) One of themselves, even a prophet of their own,
said, The Cretians are always liars, evil beasts, slow
bellies. (13) This witness is true. Wherefore rebuke them
sharply, that they may be sound in the faith; (14) not giving heed to Jewish fables, and commandments of men, that
turn from the truth. (15) Unto the pure all things are pure:
but unto them that are defiled and unbelieving is nothing
pure; but even their mind and conscience is defiled.
(16) They profess that they know God; but in works they
deny him, being abominable, and disobedient, and unto
every good work reprobate.*

Verse 12. Even though Paul softened the blow by
quoting another person, he wrote a scathing criticism of
the Cretans in general. Nations tend to have certain
characteristics, including certain virtues and vices, that
individuals tend to adopt as part of their culture and environment. Apparently the Cretans were well known in
the ancient world for three vices in particular. It seems
that false teachers found a fertile field for their seeds of
deceit.

The "prophet" Paul quoted was probably the poet
Epimenides, circa 630 B.C. Paul did not mean that this
man was a prophet of God but simply that he was a
recognized authority among the Cretans themselves.

"Always" comes from *aei,* meaning "incessantly,

perpetually, habitually." Lying seemed to be synonymous with Cretans; in the vernacular of that day "to speak like a Cretan" meant "to lie." Another knowing poet of the times said:

> Crete, which a hundred cities doth maintain,
> Cannot deny this, though to lying given.

"Evil beasts" connotes rudeness, brutality. Both Jude 10 and II Peter 2:12 mention people who are "brute beasts." Epimenides is said to have stated sarcastically that "the absence of wild beasts from Crete was supplied by its inhabitants."

"Slow bellies" is also translated "lazy gluttons" (NIV, RSV, NEB). Gluttony is intemperance in the gratification of appetite, and these Cretans seemed to personify the term.

Verse 13. Paul agreed with this assessment of the general Cretan lifestyle. In understanding and love, however, he requested Titus to provide sharp rebuke (*elegoho apotomos*) for them so that they would see the error of their way and repent. Reproof without a provision for realignment is not the Christian way. It is sound practice to rebuke to the extent necessary to evoke the appropriate response. Those who are more crusty may need a stiffer blow, while the more sensitive often respond well to a softer touch. The rebellious teachers had found easy marks among the Cretan sluggards, with both groups deserving sharp rebuke. Whatever it takes to cause us to be "sound in the faith" is merited. Soft pedaling in the matter of heresy is not the answer. Compromise never vanishes by ignoring it.

Concerning the Cretan culture, Erdman injected a cogent observation: "It is to the glory of Christianity that in soil so unpromising it produced the flower and fruit of faith and holiness."[3] We should commend Christians who flourish in such harsh environments, as did the saints in "Caesar's household" (Philippians 4:22).

Verse 14. Jewish fables—idle, foolish speculations—were also part of the problem. Paul had previously warned Timothy of such Jewish fantasies (I Timothy 1:4). The "commandments of men" are probably arbitrary prohibitions concerning ascetic life such as in Colossians 2:22. They are not required by God but are of human origin. Focusing on such things only turns people from the truth.

Verse 15. The statements here are to be understood in context, relevant to the ascetic restrictions mentioned in verse 14. The purpose of this verse is to refute legalistic, ascetic attitudes, perhaps stemming from a form of Jewish Gnosticism. To those who are pure minded, the daily activities and objects of life are pure, but carnal people taint everything they do with evil. When they try to be religious they invent all sorts of prohibitions based on their defiled conscience and their improper conduct in relation to otherwise innocent things. Blailock stated:

> Gnosticism, the multiform perversion of Christianity which was emerging at the moment, had this in common with Judaism, that it was beginning to list a mass of taboos, to call the body, marriage, and other natural practices of man "unclean." Paul's point is that no one can in any way define sin, unless he begins with a life committed to God. To evil men everything they touch, every

human practice, joy, function, becomes evil. Horace, the Roman poet, had said a century before: "Unless the vessel be clean, whatever you pour into it becomes sour." A dirty mind soils all life. If a man keeps his mind, as Isaiah put it, "stayed on God," his conscience and judgment are steadied and purified. If the "light that is in man, is itself darkness," as the Lord warned, no right decision in any moral question is possible.[4]

Evil minds may become so perverted that it is impossible for them to discriminate between what is innocent and what is bestial. God did put a "difference between holy and unholy, and between clean and unclean" (Leviticus 10:10), but He was specific in His definitions; the context reveals His intentions. Both the Jews and the Gnostics loved to enlarge on God's commandments and write a few of their own. Jesus condemned this practice soundly in Matthew 15:9 and 16:12.

Verse 16. Such people may profess to know God, but their works and words betray them as surely as did Peter's (Matthew 26:73) and the Ephraimites' (Judges 12:5-6).

To profess but not possess is acute self-deception or blatant hypocrisy. Works must substantiate our words, else we may likewise become "abominable, and disobedient, and . . . reprobate." "Reprobate" is from *adikomos,* meaning "disqualified, disapproved, worthless."

To know God by ritual alone is to know only shadow, not substance. We do not experience God only in a cup or a wafer, nor merely in a song and dance. If all we know of God is to experience goose bumps when the choir sings on Sunday night, we do not really know Him. Paul was willing to know Him "in the power of his resurrection, and the fellowship of his sufferings" (Philippians 3:10). Empty profession is as worthless as a handful of sand in the Sahara.

Footnotes

[1]D. Edmond Hiebert, *Titus and Philemon* (Chicago: Moody Press, 1957), 33.

[2]Ibid., 37.

[3]Erdman, 155.

[4]E. M. Blailock, *The Pastoral Epistles* (Grand Rapids: Zondervan, 1972), 77-78.

TITUS
Chapter Two

IV. Instructions to Various Groups in the Church (2:1-10)

A. The Older Men (2:1-2)
(1) But speak thou the things which become sound doctrine; (2) that the aged men be sober, grave, temperate, sound in faith, in charity, in patience.

Verse 1. This passage, which describes conduct expected of Christians, contrasts strikingly with the preceding verses. Regardless of what vices were rampant, what philosophical errors were in vogue, or what some professing Christians thought of his teaching, Titus was to hold to and proclaim sound doctrine. "Sound doctrine" not only relates to theology but to lifestyle, as the context reveals.

A similar exhortation was given to Timothy in I Timothy 6:11—"But thou, O man of God, flee these things." In other words, "Despite what others are doing, here is the path for you." Leadership must always set the example.

Verse 2. The instructions to be disseminated by Titus are categorized by age and gender. The first group to be admonished are the older men of the congregation. "Aged men" refers to men of mature age rather than to an office.

These men are to be revered as pillars of the assembly, but to be counted worthy of such esteem they must be sober, or self-controlled. Second, they are to be grave, meaning dignified, serious, honorable. They are to carry themselves with dignity and graceful bearing. (See I Timothy 3:8.) Third, they are to be temperate, meaning sensible, exercising self-restraint. In all areas of life they are to curb impulses toward unbridled indulgence. Fourth, they must manifest spiritual soundness in faith, Christian love, and endurance. A robust faith keeps one's eye trained on the goal; a healthy love maintains a right spirit even when wronged; a hardy patience allows one to endure the hardships of life with spiritual steadfastness.

B. The Older Women (2:3)

(3) The aged women likewise, that they be in behaviour as becometh holiness, not false accusers, not given to much wine, teachers of good things.

Verse 3. As joint heirs of the grace of life, the elderly women must also manifest character traits becoming to holiness. Their reverent demeanor marks them as examples for the younger women. *Katastema,* here translated "behaviour," includes bearing, dress, speech, and adornment. The depreciation of age does not exempt them from manifesting reverence in daily deportment and personal attire.

"False accusers" is translated from a word sometimes used of the devil or devilment, and it refers to slander.

The devil falsely accuses the brethren (Revelation 12:10), and to be caught up in talebearing or scandal-mongering is to be involved in devilment. (See I Timothy 3:11.)

"Not given to much wine" does not mean they can be given to some wine. It is simply a way to say they should not be controlled by alcohol.

They are to be "teachers of good [virtuous] things."

C. The Younger Women (2:4-5)

(4) That they may teach the young women to be sober, to love their husbands, to love their children, (5) to be discreet, chaste, keepers at home, good, obedient to their own husbands, that the word of God be not blasphemed.

Verse 4. The older women, who are to be teachers of good things, have objects for their instruction—the younger women. Ecclesiastical peace and effectiveness are in some measure dependent on domestic stability. To reinforce the stability of the home, the older women are to instruct the younger ones in several specific virtues. They are the natural ones to render this instruction rather than the husbands, the fathers, or even the elders. This type of teaching (*sophronizo,* to train, to school) is best done in the home, and as much by example as by word.

The young woman is to be sober, to exercise self-control. She is to love her husband and children. They are her first responsibility.

Verse 5. The list for young women continues. "Discreet" means sensible, careful to demonstrate godliness. It is the same word translated as "temperate" in verse 2. "Chaste" is the manifestation of purity. "Keepers at home" is the rendering of *oikourgos*—caring for the home, working at home. This activity contrasts with that of the busybody of I Timothy 5:13. The home is the Christian woman's basic sphere of loving labor, the first priority for her attributes and unique abilities. If she neglects her responsibilities in this area to compete in the marketplace, she may find her life unfulfilled and stressful. Happy is the woman who is involved in the ministry of homemaker. (See also I Timothy 5:14.)

The young woman should be "good"—showing kindness to her family and visitors. "Obedient" is from *hupotasso* and describes the attitude of submission to her husband's family leadership. (See Ephesians 5:22-24; I Peter 3:1, 5.) "That the word of God be not blasphemed" probably refers to the entire list, rather than only to the immediately previous item. Should these virtues not be taught and manifested in the Christian women, the entire gospel would become suspect. The character of its women is still a prime criterion when the world passes judgment on the church. Paul was concerned that no one conclude that Christian women make less faithful wives and mothers because of their spiritual liberty.

D. The Younger Men (2:6-8)

(6) Young men likewise exhort to be sober minded. (7) In all things shewing thyself a pattern of good works: in doctrine showing uncorruptness, gravity, sincerity, (8) sound speech, that cannot be condemned: that he that is of the contrary part may be ashamed, having no evil thing to say of you.

Verse 6. Paul did not omit the young men from his admonitions. The same disciplines are "likewise" expected from them. They too are to be sober—sensible or self-controlled. Self-control is one of the most admirable character traits, especially in youth.

Verse 7. Since Titus was probably in this age group he was to be a model—"pattern"—for the others. Thus following qualities are expected of ministers specifically and of all young Christian men. Titus was to be uncorrupted in doctrinal teaching, grave (dignified, serious, honorable), and sincere.

Verse 8. He was also to guard his speech, keeping it healthy and beyond reproach. By exhibiting these characteristics he would not only set a good example for other young men, but no opponent would be able to justifiably condemn him. Instead, such a person would be ashamed in the face of this testimony. (See I Timothy 4:12.)

E. The Servants (2:9-10)

(9) Exhort servants to be obedient unto their own masters, and to please them well in all things; not answering again; (10) not purloining, but shewing all good fidelity; that they may adorn the doctrine of God our Saviour in all things.

Verse 9. The apostle added one more category in his comprehensive exhortation—slaves. Perhaps some of all the other groups were a part of this contingent, which was based on neither age nor gender but social status. (For a discussion of slavery in New Testament times, see the commentary on I Timothy 6:1-2.) In Paul's day, slaves constituted a substantial element of the church. The welfare of the faith demanded that they be obedient to their masters, seek to please them, and not talk back disrespectfully to them.

Verse 10. Moreover, they were not to pilfer or embezzle (purloin) but manifest a trustworthiness deserving of praise. These instructions are applicable to employees, particularly in today's world when mean-spirited, greedy employees and employers are at each other's throats on the job and in the courts.

The motive for such attitudes is "that they may adorn [*kosmeo,* to embellish with honor] the doctrine of God our Saviour in all things." No master would be impressed with an employee's Christian testimony unless it was substantiated by faithfulness and loyalty. The gospel would be unattractive to the unbelieving master unless the believing slave exemplified its principles in his life. Even in the lowly duties of a slave, it was possible to glorify God with a pattern of behavior beyond reproach.

As in 1:3, this verse speaks of "God our Saviour." Like 1:4, 2:13 specifically identifies Jesus as the Savior. Clearly, Jesus is the one God incarnate.

V. The Motivation for Committed Christian Living (2:11-15)

A. The Appearance of God's Grace (2:11)
(11) For the grace of God that bringeth salvation hath appeared to all men.

Verse 11. Here is why Christians live uprightly: the saving grace of God has brought mercy instead of justice into our lives, and gratitude has provided the motivation to live above the corruption of the world (verse 12). This grace has clearly made known the will of God to all people as it relates to our association with the world around us. It brings salvation (*soterios*) from the Fall and puts us in a right standing with God.

B. The Teaching of God's Grace (2:12-13)

(12) Teaching us that, denying ungodliness and worldly lusts, we should live soberly, righteously, and godly, in this present world; (13) looking for that blessed hope, and the glorious appearing of the great God and our Saviour Jesus Christ.

Verse 12. Grace teaches the believer to respect and protect his position in Christ, willingly separating himself from the sinful practices of the unsaved. By God's grace, he can and must deny impious and worldly lusts and live soberly (sensibly), righteously, and godly (piously). Grace does not condone or cover sin; it teaches holiness (Romans 6:1-2, 15).

If conducting one's affairs blamelessly in the light of grace is unattainable, would such a command as this be in the Scriptures? We are to live this way "in this present world"—the age or time in which we now live. Indeed, by the power of the indwelling Holy Spirit, we can enjoy freedom from guilt and condemnation as we live for God, fulfill the righteousness taught by the law, and continually kill the deeds of the flesh (Romans 8:1, 4, 13). When we sit at the feet of amazing grace, discipleship is learned. Hope is engendered. Truth is ingested. Bitterness is displaced by love. Cynicism is washed away in the tide of understanding. Jesus has saved us, He is keeping us, and He is coming again to resurrect and translate us!

Verse 13. Hope feeds our endurance. It steadies our grip on grace. It buoys our spirits when circumstances are contrary. It averts our eyes from the temptations around us. "We are saved by hope" (Romans 8:24). The "blessed," or ultimate, hope is that Jesus will soon come to take His bride away. This hope keeps our knees bent, our hearts humbled, and our eyes heavenward. We are eagerly expectant, ready to welcome our Redeemer! "For the Lord Himself ["the great God and our Saviour Jesus Christ"] shall descend from heaven with a shout, with the voice of the archangel, and with the trump of God: and the dead in Christ shall rise first: then we which are alive and remain shall be caught up together with them in the clouds, to meet the Lord in the air: and so shall we ever be with the Lord" (I Thessalonians 4:16-17).

Titus 2:13 contains an obvious reference to the deity of Jesus Christ. The entire phrase, "The great God and our Saviour Jesus Christ" refers to one divine being who manifested Himself in human form for the purpose of redeeming humanity from sin. The Greek text uses only one definite article, signifying that both designations refer to one being. Therefore the NIV says, "Our great God and Savior, Jesus Christ." The great God is our Savior, Jesus Christ! There are not two deities, or two divine "persons," but there is one person, Jesus Christ, who is spirit and flesh, God and man, the Father in the Son. "God was manifest [made known] in the flesh" (I Timothy 3:16). (See also the commentary on I Timothy 1:1, 17.)

C. The Effects of God's Grace (2:14)
(14) Who gave himself for us, that he might redeem us from all iniquity, and purify unto himself a peculiar people, zealous of good works.

Verse 14. The purpose of the Incarnation was for our God and Savior to give Himself for us, redeeming us from iniquity (Galatians 3:13; 4:5; I Peter 1:18). Bethlehem was the incarnation of God—God *with* us (Matthew 1:23). Calvary was the place of sacrifice—God *for* us (Hebrews 9:27-28). Pentecost was the infusion of His power—God *in* us (Colossians 1:27).

God's purpose was not only to redeem but to purify, so that He could once again have the fellowship with holy humans that was broken by the Fall. He has achieved this purpose in the church. "Ye are a chosen generation, a royal priesthood, an holy nation, a peculiar people; that ye should shew forth the praises of him who hath called you out of darkness into his marvellous light" (I Peter 2:9). "Peculiar" in this context does not mean "strange"; rather it means "unique, a private possession, His only, belonging to none other." By character and conduct, God's people are to show that they belong wholly to Him. Being "zealous of good works" is expressive of this ownership. He who eagerly awaits His return will "occupy" (Luke 19:13), staying busy in profitable pursuits until his Lord returns!

D. The Continuity of God's Grace (2:15)
(15) These things speak, and exhort, and rebuke with all authority. Let no man despise thee.

Verse 15. The chapter concludes by reiterating the charge to the minister to faithfully teach these principles of the faith with all the authority vested in him. "Exhort" indicates that he is to make application of these teachings. "Rebuke" involves insuring that any neglectful hearers feel the force of the instructions. Conviction is the natural and expected product of reproof. The purpose of conviction is to evoke repentance and a renewed commitment to Christ.

In proclaiming these instructions for Christian living, the minister should not give cause for anyone to "despise" him. Instead of *kataphroneo,* "to look down upon," as in I Timothy 4:12, this verse uses *periphroneo,* "to think around." This word indicates a disregard of the teachings by someone who rationalizes that he is in a position beyond responsibility for these requirements, thus justifying continuance in his old ways. The minister should not condone such a rejection of his authority to expound apostolic, biblical truths.

TITUS
Chapter Three

VI. Responsibilities of the Church (3:1-11)

A. To Be Subject to Authorities (3:1)
(1) Put them in mind to be subject to principalities and powers, to obey magistrates, to be ready to every good work.

Verse 1. The emphasis now shifts to the Christian's responsibility to government and society. In view of the tendency of Cretans to resist civil control and hard work (1:12), the apostle was careful to underscore the need to submit to civil authorities. Other epistles give similar injunctions (Romans 13:1-7; I Peter 3:8-17). "Them" means all the Christians on Crete, and by extension, all believers everywhere. Chapter 2 addresses several groups of saints individually, but this chapter includes them all in its admonition.

"Principalities" (*arche*) indicates the first in a series, the "first ones" or chief rulers in a town. "Powers" are simply those exercising duly constituted authority. The "magistrates" are perhaps comparable to our modern judges, ruling in legal matters, settling disputes, and levying fines.

Christians are not to be anarchists. The principle of

government is of God. Those who rule do so with God's permission (John 19:10-11; Romans 13:1-7). They do not always do what is right (Proverbs 29:2), but they should be obeyed as long as the laws they enforce do not forbid believers to do God's will or coerce believers to sin. Christians may deem some laws good or bad, depending on their impact on the cause of God or on certain elements of society. Christians may work peacefully to change officeholders or laws, but they should not break laws in that pursuit. Respect for the legal system of government is the obligation of every believer. We are to "live peaceably with all men" (Romans 12:18). In the interest of good government, we should pray for those in power (I Timothy 2:1-3).

Being "ready to every good work" refers primarily to spiritual pursuits rather than civic endeavors. Christians sometimes are called on to serve in some civil capacity or other and may do so effectively, but participation in the political process is often risky, for in that arena one's morals and ethics are frequently tested. A Christian politician is highly visible and is likely to have any personal failings played out in the media or in the courts for all to see. In such an event the whole church may be derided and condemned.

B. To Show Brotherly Kindness (3:2)
(2) To speak evil of no man, to be no brawlers, but gentle, showing all meekness unto all men.

Verse 2. It is important for Christians to show respect for others—"do not slander, abstain from fighting, forbear, deal courteously with one another." Perhaps one purpose of the verse is to teach that Christians should not insist on their legal rights to the extent of committing moral wrong. (See I Corinthians 6:1-8.) Meekness an is unassuming spirit of humility and gentleness as opposed to self-assertiveness or haughtiness. Such an attitude is to be directed "toward all men," not only to those of the household of faith.

C. To Give Because We Have Received (3:3-7)

(3) For we ourselves also were sometimes foolish, disobedient, deceived, serving divers lusts and pleasures, living in malice and envy, hateful, and hating one another. (4) But after that the kindness and love of God our Saviour toward man appeared, (5) not by works of righteousness which we have done, but according to his mercy he saved us, by the washing of regeneration, and renewing of the Holy Ghost; (6) which he shed on us abundantly through Jesus Christ our Saviour; (7) that being justified by his grace, we should be made heirs according to the hope of eternal life.

Verse 3. Lest the Cretans resent his sharp references to their national reputation, Paul alluded to his own disgraceful past—"we ourselves also were . . ." Indeed, no Christian has anything to boast of, "for all have sinned" (Romans 3:23). A simple testimony of God's grace is one thing, but to glory in the sin one has committed is quite another. Paul seemed to blush when he spoke of his own pride and foolishness before his conversion. Some things he never shared with us, and what he did share was always in the context of the Lord's mercy. "Let not the wise man glory in his wisdom, neither let the mighty man glory in his might, let not the rich man glory in his riches: but let him that glorieth glory in this, that he understandeth and knoweth me, that I am the LORD which exercise lovingkindness, judgment, and righteousness, in the earth: for in these things I delight, saith the LORD" (Jeremiah 9:23-24).

A sordid past blotted out by the blood of Christ is sufficient motivation to treat others kindly, to live above reproach, and to demonstrate meekness. "There, but for the grace of God, go I." Paul enumerated his own misdeeds, calling them "foolish"—a stronger word in the Bible than in its general meaning today. (See Psalm 14:1; 73:22; Romans 1:21; I Corinthians 1:18; Ephesians 5:15.) Foolishness in the biblical sense tends to mental perversion, the natural result being disobedience and deception. One becomes a veritable slave to base desires and pleasures, living only for their fulfillment. Malice, an evil attitude of ill-will and even a desire to injure, and envy, its cousin, which detests the good fortune of others, follow along after such behavior, affording a still deeper pit for the sinner. One comes to hate others because he hates himself, realizing the detestable state of his own life.

As Lilley put it: "Sin blunts the mind (foolish), perverts the heart and will (disobedient, going astray), stimulates carnal desires (lusts, pleasures), and encourages the growth of all forms of selfish feeling (malice, envy, hate)."[1]

Verse 4. What a difference the little word "but" makes! That was the way we were, but! We were forever doomed, but! But the kindness of God was revealed, the way of escape was made, the door of hope was opened! Praise God, the story did not end with verse 3! Verses 4-6 are the "rest of the story!"

226

"Love toward man" is *philanthropia,* from *phileo,* "to love" and *anthropos,* the general term for "mankind." The "so great salvation" (Hebrews 2:3) provided for all humanity was purely the result of the goodness of God— the Divine Philanthropist! No human attribute made us deserving of such a provision. God's boundless generosity has always been a reality, but the verb "appeared," used also in 2:11, indicates that these attributes were revealed clearly in the work of Christ and in the subsequent preaching of the gospel. The God of Abraham, Isaac, and Jacob indeed became "God our Saviour."

Verse 5. God saved us by His mercy, not on the basis of our works. "Not by works" corresponds with Ephesians 2:8-9: "For by grace are ye saved through faith; and that not of yourselves: it is the gift of God: not of works, let any man should boast." Is the context of the Pastoral Epistles an appropriate setting for such a statement, when all around it the seeming preoccupation with "good works" is in evidence? Are the Epistles at odds with each other? On the contrary, the two ideas are in perfect agreement! When a person comes to God for salvation, he has nothing to bring but faith. Good works, human righteousness, feeding the hungry, providing for the poor, being basically an honest and moral person, and so on are but "filthy rags" in the sight of God (Isaiah 64:6). Such deeds cannot earn salvation; salvation is by faith alone, lest a person boast of what he has done in order to secure it.

Faith includes trust, reliance, and obedience to the One in whom we believe. It motivates a person to seek forgiveness for sins and the impartation of new life, leading him to repentance, to the waters of baptism in humble obedience, and to the infilling of the Holy Spirit

(Mark 16:16; John 7:37-39; Acts 2:38; I Peter 3:21). Is saving faith really present when obedience is absent? If a person says, "I have faith in the shed blood of Jesus Christ," but refuses to take up his cross daily and follow Him, can he truly be a disciple? (Luke 14:26-33).

Our salvation experience, or new birth, originates in God's mercy, or grace. We receive it by faith. It consists of "the washing of regeneration, and renewing of the Holy Ghost."

"Washing" is *loutron,* derived from *louo*—"to bathe the whole body"—and is used here instead of *nipto,* which means to wash only a part of the body such as the hands or face. It is found only here and in Ephesians 5:26, where it is incorporated in the phrase "the washing of water by the word." Weymouth translates the phrase in Titus 3:5 as "the bath of regeneration." In the new-birth experience God washes all our sins away. This washing away, or remission, of sins occurs at repentance and water baptism (Acts 2:38; 22:16).

The baptism of the Holy Spirit is also part of the new-birth experience. Here the emphasis is not only on the initial work of the Holy Spirit in regeneration but also on the continuing, progressive work of sanctification ("renewing"), which begins at that point. Regeneration is a one-time event; renewing is a daily process (II Corinthians 4:16; Colossians 3:10). The coming of the Holy Spirit into the lives of believers, the seal of the new covenant (Ephesians 1:13), produces newness: "newness of life" (Romans 6:4); "newness of spirit" (Romans 7:6); "a new heart and a new spirit" (Ezekiel 18:31); "new tongues" (Mark 16:17); "a new lump" (I Corinthians 5:7); "a new creature . . . all things are become new" (II Corinthians 5:17); "the new man, which is renewed in knowledge after the image of him that created him" (Colossians 3:10). The new person lives by a "new commandment" (John 13:34; I John 2:8), possesses an inheritance under the "new covenant" (Hebrews 8:13; 12:24), will receive a "new name" (Revelation 3:12), will sing a "new song" (Revelation 5:9), and will dwell in the "new Jerusalem" (Revelation 21:2).

Verse 6. In view of our totally new life through the Spirit, it is no wonder that Paul described the Holy Spirit by the following phrase: "which he [God] shed on us abundantly." This terminology points specifically to the outpouring or baptism of the Holy Spirit (Acts 10:45; 11:15-17).

Our salvation was purchased by the death of Jesus Christ on the cross. Our faith must wholly be in the efficacy of the blood of Jesus Christ. We must believe in our hearts that He died for our sins, that He was buried, and that God raised Him from the dead (Romans 10:9; I Corinthians 15:1-4, 14). We must accept His death as our own (Romans 5:6-8). Only by His blood and by faith in His blood can we be born again. His blood enables us to repent, washes away our sins at baptism, and enables us to receive the Holy Spirit.

Verse 7. In short, we are "justified" (counted as righteous) by God's grace. As used here, the word embraces the whole work of the grace of Christ in the heart of the believer to prepare him for eternal life. Based on this justification, we qualify to become "heirs of God, and joint-heirs with Christ" (Romans 8:17; Galatians 3:29; 4:7). To be an heir is to be in line for possessions handed down from the Father. In the case of the Christian, that means eternal life and glory (John 17:22-24; I Peter 3:7). We do not have the fullness now (Romans 8:23), but we do possess "the hope of eternal life" if we possess Christ, for "Christ in you [is] the hope of glory" (Colossians 1:27).

D. To Maintain Good Works (3:8)

(8) This is a faithful saying, and these things I will that thou affirm constantly, that they which have believed in God might be careful to maintain good works. These things are good and profitable unto men.

Verse 8. This verse underscores the need to regularly set before the people the practical fundamentals of the faith just spelled out. To "affirm" is to teach strongly. The minister is to teach these principles constantly, and the believers are to take care, or thought, to maintain and compliment them.

"Good works" are the positive elements of the Christian's relationships to other believers, the government, and the unsaved. Believers are to spend their time in pursuits that benefit others, build up the household of faith, and bring glory to God. This admonition sets the stage for the one that follows.

E. To Avoid Useless Controversies and Contentions (3:9)

(9) But avoid foolish questions, and genealogies, and contentions, and strivings about the law; for they are unprofitable and vain.

Verse 9. Discussion of foolish questions is the pastime of the ignorant, who profess themselves to be wise

(Romans 1:22). Asking questions that are irrelevant or that have no scriptural answers is useless and is dangerous if pursued to the point of contention. Examples of such questions that theologians have debated are: How many angels can dance on the head of a pin? Did Adam have a navel? What will become of pregnant women in the Rapture? Will we wear shoes in heaven? Interesting enough to the unlearned, such questions are without profit to the Christian. The Greek word *moros* (stupid, dull, the source of our word *moron*) is translated "foolish."

Many Jews of Paul's day delighted in such frivolous "questions." Pride of race also motivated them to establish their lineage and boast of it. Perhaps some had so little godliness in their own lives that they sought the harder to find it in their ancestors. No doubt they could spin endless stories about the exploits of their forebears. Certainly they filled many volumes with their "contentions, and strivings about the law." The Talmud is a library of books containing the whole body of the Jewish civil and canonical laws and traditions with the commentaries and speculations of the rabbis. Many of these ideas existed before Christ came, as the oral law of the Jews. While the Talmud contains moral and ethical teachings and sheds light on Jewish thinking and customs, much of it concerns trivial, minute, obscure rabbinical interpretations and disputes that are "unprofitable and vain." Christians should avoid strife and fighting over matters such as these. (See also I Timothy 1:4-7; II Timothy 2:23.)

F. To Reject Divisive Persons (3:10-11)

(10) A man that is an heretick after the first and second admonition reject; (11) knowing that he that is such is subverted, and sinneth, being condemned of himself.

Verse 10. By definition, a heretic (*hairetikos,* factious person) is one who is quarrelsome and stirs up factions through erroneous opinions. In other words, he chooses his own way over God's way and contends for his ideas to the disunity of the body. His theology is unsound. He may even receive "revelations" to support his contentions. Paul gave Timothy clear instructions on how to handle such a person (I Timothy 6:3-5). Here he told Titus to warn a heretic once, and if need be, twice. If he still persists in his ways, he is to be avoided, other members of the church having no Christian fellowship with him. Such persons love the limelight and attention that their contentions attract, and to take it away is perhaps the only way to deal effectively with them. Moreover, their insistence on promoting false, divisive doctrine leaves no basis for fellowship. Continued acceptance of them as members of the church would only promote their dangerous influence.

Verse 11. If the divisive person will not cease and desist after the first and second admonition, it becomes obvious that he is "subverted" (*ektrepo,* to turn or twist out) and has become perverse. It reveals that his heart has been affected and that his positions are not merely mental miscalculations. His persistent contention and his refusal to heed wise counsel from his spiritual authority make him a sinner. By his actions, he passes adverse judgment upon himself—"condemned of himself."

VII. Conclusion (3:12-15)

A. Replacements for Titus (3:12)
(12) When I shall send Artemas unto thee, or Tychicus, be diligent to come unto me to Nicopolis: for I have determined there to winter.

Verse 12. Paul's final instructions to Titus included plans for replacing him on Crete. Of Artemas we know nothing further. One tradition says he was later the bishop of Lystra. Tychicus is mentioned several times in Paul's writings (Ephesians 6:21; Colossians 4:7; II Timothy 4:12) and was the bearer of several of Paul's epistles. He became Timothy's relief in Ephesus. When his replacement did come, Titus was to join Paul in Nicopolis, in eastern Macedonia, where he purposed to spend the winter.

B. Assistance for Workers on Their Journey (3:13-14)

(13) Bring Zenas the lawyer and Apollos on their journey diligently, that nothing be wanting unto them. (14) And let ours also learn to maintain good works for necessary uses, that they be not unfruitful.

Verse 13. Paul asked Titus to aid Zenas and Apollos on their mission, which was evidently assigned by Paul. This verse gives us a glimpse of the apostle as a spiritual strategist who knew how to best utilize the human resources at his disposal. Evidently these Christian brothers had brought the letter to Titus. Now he was to supply whatever was necessary to speed them on their journey. Assisting Christian workers on their journey is a biblical principle (Romans 15:24; I Corinthians 16:6, 11; II Corinthians 1:16).

Zenas is mentioned only here, and the verse does not say whether the law he practiced was Greek or Roman. It may have been that he was a former Jewish scribe and merely retained the designation of lawyer after his conversion. He is the only Christian lawyer mentioned in the Bible. In the third century Hippolytus identified him as one of the Seventy and afterwards bishop of Diospolis.

Apollos was the brilliant orator from Alexandria converted by Aquila and Priscilla who subsequently did a commendable work in Corinth (Acts 18:24-28). He became an associate of Paul in his work (I Corinthians 16:12), although Paul had to quell a party spirit in Corinth because of Apollos's popularity when he labored there (I Corinthians 1:12, 3:4-6; 22, 4:6). Their continued cooperation shows that there was no jealousy in Paul's heart toward the popular preacher and that there was no significant difference in their teachings.

Verse 14. Not only did Paul ask Titus to meet the need of the missionaries, Paul told him to make sure that the Cretan Christians had the opportunity to help supply the need. Such assistance would be "good works for necessary uses." They would thereby learn to be useful to the kingdom of God, and in doing so, they would not be "unfruitful." Pastors need to teach saints to have a missionary burden, give generously, be hospitable, and support other ministries.

C. Benediction (3:15)

(15) All that are with me salute thee. Greet them that love us in the faith. Grace be with you all. Amen.

Verse 15. Paul's companions sent their greetings. He did not name them, evidently depending on Zenas and Apollos to do so in their greeting. Paul's greeting was to be passed on to the Cretan Christians—"them that love us in the faith." Doubtless the faithful did love him, but the heretics did not.

Paul closed on a note of grace evident throughout the epistle. He wished that the benefits of God's grace would abound in all of their lives. "Amen" ends the prayer, requesting simply, "Let it be so."

Footnote

[1]J. P. Lilley, "The Pastoral Epistles," *Handbook for Bible Classes* (Edinburgh: T. & T. Clark, 1901), 255.